Church Be Nimble

Organizational Dynamics and Creativity in Mainline Congregations

Marty Kuchma

Church Be Nimble Publications

Church Be Nimble:
Organizational Dynamics and Creativity
In Mainline Congregations

Additional Information is available at:
www.churchbenimble.com.

ISBN-13: 9780692028407
ISBN-10: 0692028404

Printed by CreateSpace

Cover Layout by Lucy

For my girls

Table of Contents

Acknowledgements

This book has been a lifetime in the making. It begins and ends with the dual realization that I love the Church enough to have committed my life to ordained ministry, but, in so many ways, church bureaucracy drives me absolutely bonkers. Far too often, it seems that "the way we've always done it" sits right in the way of God doing awesome new things. I hope to change that with what is written here.

I am grateful for and to all who have helped me become who I am and allowed me to see the great goodness in life, those who have broadened my perspective, sparked my curiosity, strengthened my resolve. Though I cannot list them all here, their names are forever etched in my memory and written on my heart.

I am thankful to have been born into a family that has nurtured me in durable bonds of love and, from my earliest recollections, encouraged lively faith to carry me along what has been a rich spiritual journey that continues still.

This book is the product of varied experiences with churches which include feeling an undeniable call to the priesthood at the age of ten and almost becoming a Benedictine monk after sixteen years of Catholic school, then living for years in the spiritual wilderness serving my "congregation" of children, families and staff with whom I worked as an agnostic clinical social worker, supervisor, administrator and consultant. Along the way, I have spent time meaningfully engaged with Presbyterians and United Methodists and I continue to enjoy opportunities for ecumenical and interfaith involvement. After a wonderfully transformative period of "sanctuary" with the Unitarian Universalists, Andover Newton Theological School helped me find my way to the United Church of Christ as a comfortable place for me within mainline Protestantism.

I am blessed to be senior pastor of the most awesome congregation in the world, St. Paul's United Church of Christ in Westminster, Maryland. With love and faithfulness, they have nurtured me in ministry and given me time and the opportunity to invest in this study. They actively participated in trials during the early stages of the dissertation out of which this book emerged and graciously granted me a sabbatical during the most intense period of writing.

More broadly, that congregation supported my completion of the Doctor of Ministry program at Lancaster Theological Seminary where I came into contact with so many amazing people. In particular, I am deeply grateful to Dr. Anabel Proffitt who encouraged me to wonder and indeed wandered with me through this project from beginning to end, sharing her vast treasure of resources and ideas along with heavy doses of enthusiasm and encouragement. As the project began in earnest, Dr. David Mellott brought important insights and wise guidance to the team, offering just the right mix of validation and challenging observations that sharpened the project's focus and final presentation. Together, they made this book much better than I could have ever managed on my own.

Over time, this project has become a collective work that has been influenced by the many students who have participated in classes based on this material and the many others who have been involved in related presentations and workshops in various settings. Each experience has given me an opportunity to re-think and revise, and each has absolutely rekindled my passion for this work. The people I have encountered along the way have bolstered my determination to get this book into the world.

While so many have contributed to this book, what is written here is mine, of course, for better or worse.

My daughters, Lucy and Meg, to whom this book is dedicated, continue to keep me in touch with the utter beauty of life, and they embody my hope for the future. They and their mom, Sue Snively, have supported me throughout this project, and they have helped me in specific ways, even as our family became stronger by re-configuring over the course of this project. How my girls have grown since this project first began to take shape… May this book help strengthen the church for and with and through them, for the sake of all generations yet to come.

OPENING

A Cautionary Tale

A member of a small, Mainline congregation was inspired to help a neighbor family that lost everything to a fire that destroyed their home. The woman had a vision of her church coordinating a community effort to offer assistance. She saw it as the right thing to do, and she was hopeful that the church could pull together a larger effort than she could muster on her own.

She thought of asking the congregation's Mission Committee for help. But that committee was no longer functioning because no one agreed to serve on it. So the woman was told to raise the issue with the church's governing board – whose regularly-scheduled meeting was two weeks away. Unable to find a way around the delay, the woman used the time to work on the presentation of her proposal. But the Board had a full agenda that included sorting through roof repair estimates and planning the congregation's upcoming stewardship campaign to help fend off the latest budget shortfall.

It turned out that the time allotted for conversation about helping the neighbors was, in the end, not enough to move the matter along. Nonetheless, one of the members expressed a concern that the church's name not be attached to something the Board had not yet approved. So any official involvement by the congregation had to be put on hold.

The proposal was added to the board's agenda as "old business" for the next monthly meeting at which it became clear that the project depended on money from the church budget. Because the Mission Committee no longer existed to authorize expenditures, it became necessary for the Budget Committee to sign off on requisitions – which, of course, couldn't happen until that committee met, talked about the proposal, voted on it, and reported back to the Board.

While the woman tried to walk her proposal through her church's bureaucratic maze, luckily a number of individuals and other organizations stepped in to provide for the family's emergency needs. After a couple of months with no resolution regarding her idea, the woman finally stopped coming to Board meetings, right at about the same time she stopped coming to church.

An opportunity for ministry was missed because of the way the church was organized. The woman's proposal started as an impulse to do what one might reasonably assume Jesus would have done. Good and faithful people tried their best to do their part. Yet the process ended in a quagmire of meetings and procedural protocols that stopped a ministry opportunity in its tracks, leaving everyone feeling discouraged and defeated. Could it have been otherwise? Should it have been otherwise?

INTRODUCTION

Imagine what's possible if your congregation were to tap the wellspring of God's creative energy, discover new ways of organizing your ministry, and reach toward fresh new life with a sense of excitement and adventure.

For the past several years, as both a pastor of a local congregation and an instructor at a regional seminary, I have been engaged in an intensive study of organizational dynamics and creativity in churches. My fundamental assumption has been that organizational change is central to church revitalization and renewal because, quite simply, the way congregations organize to do their work has impact on absolutely everything else they do.

My hope throughout has been to help churches discover ways to more nimbly organize themselves for the ministry to which they feel called. Along the way, I have talked with many church people from whom I have sensed a general longing for new ways for churches to do what they do. Almost to a person, those with whom I have spoken have greeted information about my topic with some degree of apparent surprise – and an element of what seems to be a kind of hopeful curiosity. Many have asked to see what I come up with. This is it.

Since the moment this study began to take shape, I have been attentively listening in on several conversations about organizational development, dynamics, and design. Those conversations are taking place in churches and church literature, to be sure. But they are also happening in places church people have not necessarily been paying much attention, like in science labs, design firms, academic classrooms, and progressive corporate boardrooms. They include the voices of people on the cutting edge of organizational innovation who embrace creativity with gusto and let their imaginations romp playfully through this world of wonder. By opening themselves fully to discovery and delight, perhaps they have even encountered God in unique ways that others of us have missed.

What you now have in front of you is my best attempt to bring some of those voices together in one place so that you, too, can know what is being talked about and make informed choices about ways to organize your congregation for the ministry to which you feel called. I hope this material will spark your imagination, open you to exciting new possibilities, and help you move beyond the way it's always been for the sake of what might be but is not yet.

Through it all, I have become increasingly convinced of two things: First, staying the same means falling behind in a world that's always changing. Second, there are viable and valuable ways for congregations to move forward.

In the end, it matters very little whether God is still speaking or the world is radically changing if churches continue to organize themselves to always do what they've always done. What chance do fresh breezes of the Spirit have in systems designed to withstand even the mightiest winds of change?

There is a better way. Together we can find it.

Next First Steps on a Journey of Discovery

You are about to embark on a journey of discovery that will relate concepts like creativity, flexibility, and organizational agility to church life. I wonder if you have ever thought of your congregation as organizationally nimble, or if you've ever wanted or needed it to be more so.

In these pages and through all that we will do as a result of our learning together, we will delve into matters of church organization in ways that will help you realize your congregation's highest ideals and most noble purposes. By offering a means by which to re-think church organization, these reflections provide a way for vibrant ministry and meaningful discipleship to maintain or reclaim their place at the very top of your congregation's list of things to do today. We will remind ourselves of what we all know but can lose sight of amidst the myriad day-to-day pressures of congregational life: at their best, churches are merely conduits through which the love of God is shared with a world that desperately needs it. Accordingly, we will acknowledge that the institutional welfare of churches is a means to ministry but never its end. And we will consider church renewal at a most fundamental level that affects everything your congregation can and will do in the service of your unique mission.

Each person who comes to these readings will do so for their own reasons. There may be some common threads. For example, I suspect that some will come simply because they are intrigued by the possibility of new possibilities, hoping, believing that there is a better way that they just haven't found yet. May those inspired by a sense of adventure have their imaginations unleashed and their spirits set free. Others may come to this program out of fear of the things so many people in Mainline Protestant churches are concerned about these days – dramatic, decades-long declines in important numbers and cultural relevance, dire predictions about the future, worries about their own congregation's current circumstances and ultimate fate. May those motivated by fear and worry find here honest to God hope for a new day. Sheer frustration will likely bring still others to this material, frustration with trying hard to make things happen only to have their good intentions suffocate in a tangle of red tape. May those who've encountered obstacles to meaningful ministry discover a wide open field upon which to bring to life the kind of church they've been dreaming of. And some will come because someone else decided that doing so might be a good idea. May those trusting souls appreciate that they hang out in wise company. What brings you here today?

OK, that wasn't a rhetorical question. I guess now is as good a time as any to let you know that there is no place for passivity in this process. There is much for us to do during our time together, and most of the remaining work will more fruitfully be done by you than by me. You might want to keep a pencil close at hand. Or, even better, a box of crayons or markers to add a bit of color to your reflections.

So what really does bring you here today?

_____

_____

You might productively read this book on your own and find here useful insights and information. Beyond that, however, I hope you will enjoy this material with others. Built for multiple levels of involvement, these readings are ultimately designed to prompt meaningful conversation and purposeful action by groups of congregational leaders who might be elected officers and interested others, ordained and lay, life-long pillars of their church communities and new members just finding their way.

Twenty readings are provided here, and they are separated into four sections. Each reading examines a particular aspect of organizational life, and together the readings cover a broad spectrum of topics related to church organization. The first set of reflections explores factors that have influenced the development of organizational models that are now common. Lifting up tacit assumptions underlying common organizational practices allows a critical examination of their ongoing usefulness. The second set of reflections stretches the theoretical underpinnings of organizational life to include ideas from disparate fields and areas of interest, all with the hope of inspiring new ways to think about how churches might organize themselves. The third set of reflections applies innovative concepts to real-world situations; it focuses on practical ideas to ponder and play with. And the final set of reflections provides support for undertaking and sustaining organizational change in local congregations.

Two additional readings are offered as resources. The first describes a process called "Presencing" that can set the tone for approaching the work that lies ahead. The second highlights conversation as a vital tool in congregational revitalization and renewal.

Rather than merely reading the material, you are invited to reflect on each topic and add your own insights and experiences in the open spaces that are provided – or on another page or on canvas or keyboard. Now might be a good time to start a journal if writing helps you think things through. Or take a walk or make a quilt or commit to another activity that helps you make and find meaning. In all things, take time to notice God's infinitely and dazzlingly creative presence in your life and in your church. And let yourself dream of a better way.

Indeed what matters most of all is what you and your colleagues make of this invitation to pause and think again about how your congregation is organized to do its work. You are the experts in your setting, and you will find your way forward together. May this process help you explore new possibilities and make the best of this opportunity to redesign your congregation's organizational life.

As you engage this process, be sure to begin at the beginning. Avoid the trap of trying to solve problems and make plans before you really know what's happening. Be intentional about setting aside assumptions, personal agendas, and anything like pre-conceived notions. Don't try to peek at the last chapter without understanding the steps that will take you there. Instead, before leaping to conclusions, settle into this study and look at your congregation with fresh eyes through the prism of each chapter. Take time to make sense of what you really see. Be willing to be surprised. Be prepared to even be unsure of yourself from time to time. Let yourself not know what you think you know so that you can really know what's really there. Only then will you be prepared to take your next steps into the future.

In all things, remember that God is still creating, always and everywhere. May God's awe-some creative energy abound within you, among you, and all around you! And may you have the wisdom to notice…

SECTION ONE: FINDING OUR PLACE

Have you ever wondered why churches do the things they do in the ways they do them? This first section of reflections begins with the hope of illuminating some of the factors that have shaped church organization as we now know it. Knowing allows perspective, which makes it possible to approach anew what can easily be taken for granted. Through these readings, we will look at church organization through a variety of lenses, including church historical, scientific, and generational. The section works toward an assessment of the significant challenges and vital choices churches are now facing, and it concludes by taking note of specific common practices in church organization in hopes of discerning options and perceiving what else might be preferable and even possible.

1) LOOKING BACK: HOW WE GOT TO WHERE WE ARE

Try as we might to make it so, looking backward cannot show us the way forward. But it can help us understand a little more about how we got to be who we are as we move into the future. A brief historical overview can give us a sense of some of the ways church organization has developed in dialogue with the prevailing culture in various times and places throughout history, even as it reminds us that our very own congregations exist in dynamic tension with the particular historical and cultural circumstances in which we find ourselves today. With an emphasis on the early church and the Protestant Reformation, this short study might be thought of as a glimpse into the rise and the fall of a unified, centralized institutional church.

Christianity as a Movement

Let's first remember with church consultant Gil Rendle that "Christianity began as a way of life, a movement with a clear identity and purpose" (xi). The earliest Christians, before they were called Christians or anything at all, were flexibly organized around the ministry of Jesus of Nazareth who roamed the Galilean countryside preaching, teaching, healing, feeding. Organizationally nimble and free of any discernible institutional bureaucracy whatsoever, the group revolved around Jesus' mission which Luke 4:18-19 sums up this way: " to bring good news to the poor... proclaim release to the captives and recovery of sight to the blind, to let the oppressed go free, to proclaim the year of the Lord's favor."

The radical implications of their mission not only situated Jesus and his followers as outsiders who routinely questioned and criticized the established institutions of their day. That mission also required them to be in a constant process of self-discovery about how best to do what they set out to do. They were quite literally and in every way an emerging church, generating dynamic, creative energy by way of a movement that gathered momentum as it grew. But with Jesus' death, things changed.

Theologian Walter Wink writes that, "With his death, Jesus quickly entered his own myth. He became larger than life. Worship of Jesus as God soon eclipsed the arduous task of continuing his work and living his way" (137). And in important respects, lacking their leader, Jesus' followers turned their attention toward finding an organizational model that would provide safety and stability while still preserving some sense of connection with their past and their purpose. Israel Galindo writes that "rather than create a new thing suitable to contain the new creation of the Church, they used an existing congregational form – the synagogue – and shoehorned the new movement into it, even borrowing its liturgy in the practice of corporate worship" (23). In the process, they began to substitute structure for mission and form for function.

Early Christianity took various forms, including gatherings under the leadership of influential community leaders in private homes and corporate worship in often-clandestine congregate settings. It was difficult for lasting structures to really take hold, however, because in all that they did the early Christians were a persecuted lot.

But then their fate changed dramatically under Emperor Constantine who, for the good of the Roman Empire in 325 CE, embraced Christianity and moved Christians from the margins of society to the very center of imperial power. That was a pivotal moment in the development of the Christian church and it had profound implications for church organization. Indeed the significance of Christianity becoming the officially sanctioned religion of the Empire probably cannot be over-estimated on any level, including organizational.

Suddenly, this group of Christians that had, since its inception, existed in opposition to imperial authority was now on the inside of power looking out. Rather than opposing the way things were done, their change in status both made it possible for them to adopt the ways of power and compelled them to do so, lest they risk falling from favor. Slowly but surely, the newly-sanctioned church took on some of the characteristics of the establishment it had opposed. Then it took on a lot of those characteristics.

Over time, the church adopted aspects of imperial organizational models, eventually seating a pope as peer to the Emperor, and forming an elaborate hierarchy which pulled together and ordered ecclesiastical positions and offices, only some of which had begun to emerge prior to the church's ascent to prominence. Training and ordination of clergy became increasingly important and lay members were consequently relegated to subordinate roles in church life. Bishops, including the pope as Bishop of Rome, expanded their reach and asserted control over their various territories.

At times, the line between church and empire blurred completely and the church even found itself in the position of crowning secular leaders on occasion. Papal power waxed and waned according to political alliances that shifted from time to time, all against the backdrop of theological and doctrinal ferment, some of which continues to this day. Those on the "losing" side of contentious battles sometimes paid the high price of excommunication and, worse, martyrdom at the hands of the church which seized opportunities to consolidate matters of doctrine and protocol if for nothing more than institutional self-preservation. So bureaucracy was built upon bureaucracy, even to the extent that it risked overshadowing the ministry and discipleship that had always been the church's stated reason for being.

For many centuries, prescribed rites and rituals did ensure some level of unity and uniformity throughout the church. But unity and uniformity proved to be especially elusive goals into the Middle Ages, when they became virtually unattainable.

A Protestant Reformation

In 1517, Martin Luther, a Roman Catholic priest, posted his famous 95 Theses on a church door in Wittenburg, Germany, and in so doing formalized a split between the heretofore dominant Roman Catholic Church and newly emerging groups of Christians who came to be known as Protestants. Luther's bold assertion, along with the writings and actions of other reformers like John Calvin in Switzerland and others throughout Europe, precipitated a new movement within the church. The resulting Reformation moved Protestants beyond the authority of popes and bishops, abandoned or modified customary rites and rituals, and made the Bible more directly accessible to all Christians.

Of particular significance for our purposes, Luther advocated the "priesthood of all believers" and took seriously the role of non-ordained Christians in the life of the church. That severing of ties with the established institutional order and simultaneous recasting of the "priesthood" made it both possible and necessary for reformers to develop organizational models that better suited their newly-begun churches. In the process, each new "church" had the opportunity to accept or reject aspects of how things had always been done, to surmise what the Bible recommended about church organization (which is not much), and then to look further afield to government, business, and other types of organizations that might inform their efforts at institutional reconfiguration.

A wide variety of church organizational models emerged, ranging from tightly-held centralized control where church governance emanated out from a unified denominational authority, to complete congregational autonomy in which denominations speak to but not for local congregations in the context of covenantal relationships. Along the way, representational forms of church governance were also instituted, designating boards of leaders to oversee church operations in much the same fashion as modern church councils, boards, and consistories do now.

Craig Dykstra and James Hudnut-Buemler trace the evolution of mainline denominations from constitutional confederacies in the 1780's to corporations or corporate model organizations in the 1830's to 1860's, then to regulatory agencies in the 1960's (307-331). Much of the inclination toward regulation was driven by a desire, amidst increased diversity and societal turmoil, to establish norms and create parameters for behavior and belief.

Indeed church organizational models have continued to evolve, influenced by historical events and cultural trends, shaped by various movements within the church toward independence and reunification, and informed by trial and error learning in local congregations and throughout larger church bodies. Governmental, legislative, and corporate models continue to inform the organizational life of churches, and they have exerted considerable influence over contemporary church polity and governance.

QUESTION FOR REFLECTION: In what ways does your church organizational model include elements of bureaucracy that you might expect to find in government agencies, legislative bodies, or corporate settings?

There are as many ways to organize churches as there are churches to organize. There is no pre-ordained organizational model. Instead, the many variations we now have evolved in various times and places to meet specific needs in the context of cultural and historical factors, and they continue to be shaped in one way or another by underlying theological assumptions. That ongoing interactional process both invites and challenges us to develop organizational models that work for our particular circumstances.

2) LOOKING BENEATH: DISASSEMBLING NEWTON'S MACHINES

We are now on the cusp of a paradigm change in terms of organizational dynamics. The day is dawning on a worldview that conceives of organizations as living systems. Understanding the dimensions and implications of that shift and applying related ideas to church organization require that we understand some of the significant assumptions underlying the paradigm that organizations like churches are on the verge of moving beyond. Undertaking that study will require that we travel back in time a few hundred years.

In the seventeenth century, Sir Isaac Newton changed the world by claiming that all things on the earth and beyond the earth are governed by a set of principles that cause them to function in predictable ways. The principles he proposed made the world seem less mysterious and presumably more controllable. Apples fall from trees because of the same gravity that keeps the planets in their orbits. Objects set in motion remain in motion and objects at rest remain at rest until they are acted upon by equal and opposite forces to change their status. "A" predictably leads to "B" and causes "B." Even God as "the very first cause" was the object of Newton's search (Armstrong 203). For centuries, the Newtonian worldview has been a dominant paradigm that has had broad influence on organizational development and, consequently, on congregational life.

Machines

The Newtonian paradigm helped set the stage for a world of machines that powered the Industrial Revolution. Machines are conglomerations of parts positioned in relation to other parts so that sufficient force in a particular direction causes the machine to produce the same result over and over again. Lacking the capacity for spontaneous reorganization, machines are what they are and they do what they do. The only other alternative is that they are "broken" and need to be "fixed."

Unfortunately, the natural course for machines is to inevitably wear out and break down. Since machines are constantly vulnerable to the effects of deterioration and other damage, and since they lack any capacity to reinvent themselves in ways that might be adaptive, any change is a potentially destructive force. Change is at least always a disruptive force. Accordingly, machines and their operators work toward equilibrium as the optimal operating state; staying the same becomes the primary objective in a machine worldview. And because basic survival is often at stake, any deviation from equilibrium can arouse fear in those charged with machine maintenance.

When applied to church organization, because it sets equilibrium as the highest priority and emphasizes the ongoing need to combat inevitable decline, machine thinking perceives of congregations as being precariously perched on a downward slope and susceptible to dangers of all sorts. To avoid extinction, according to machine thinking, congregations must orient themselves toward staying the way they are. Given that assumption about the fragility of their own continued existence, they understandably become fearful of any variation and reluctant to try new things. So they cling to what is. Organizational consultant Margaret Wheatley writes that, "If we believe that the universe is on a relentless road to death, we can't help but live in fear of change. In a downhill world, any change exhausts our store of valuable energy and leaves us empty, one step closer to death. Staying put or keeping our balance is a means of defense against the eroding forces of nature. We want nothing to change because only decline awaits us" (Leadership 77). And most people could do without that.

From a machine model perspective, people in organizations including churches are generally viewed as inert "parts" whose functioning depends almost entirely upon external force and explicit direction. In order for the machine to stay in proper order, the capacity for creative self-expression by any of the parts must deliberately be limited. Even when people are already busily and productively engaged in a church's ministry, the organizational dynamics of the church may still demand external intervention to manage what people are up to.

In machine model organizations, it is assumed that energy and instruction must be provided by authoritative entities that serve some sort of executive function. Those entities typically operate by way of command and control leadership channeled through well-defined structures according to prescribed procedures to yield specific and predictable results. When the machine is operating properly, energy is put into the machine, works its way through the machine according to a predetermined sequence, and comes out on the other side in the form of the desired product. In churches, this dynamic is played out, for example, when one person or committee with authority instructs another person or committee to carry out a particular function or work toward a specific goal.

When deterioration or damage occurs in organizations operating under machine model assumptions, parts are simply removed, repaired or replaced as needed so that the machine can resume doing what it was doing before the problems arose. Benjamin Zander notes that, "Because the model is based on the assumption that life will be under control if everyone plays his part, when things do break down, someone or something naturally gets blamed" (145). For example, perceived problems might be addressed by replacing this chairperson or that one, or by drawing new lines of accountability between new blocks on an organizational chart, or by other such attempts to "fix problems" and restore the machine to the *status quo*. It has even been the case that failure to reach certain predetermined goals or expectations has resulted in the replacement of pastors based on the often-erroneous assumption that changing out that one part of the machine structure will make all things right again.

Those types of intervention are appropriate if one ignores the dynamic interdependence of all of the parts with each other and with the wider world. Machine models discount the importance of the relationship networks that underlie all human organizations. Removing, repairing and replacing parts to fix problems also assumes that parts are unquestionably interchangeable and that all people who might occupy the various blocks of the organizational chart are essentially the same, lacking any meaningful unique characteristics, gifts, passions, or hopes. Instead, they are dealt with as cogs in a lifeless contraption.

While machine model thinking may be perfectly adequate for understanding machines, it does not translate well to working with living organisms and organizations, including congregations.

Moving On

Machine-model assumptions have provided a sense of comfort and security which is reinforced by the promise of predictability. They attempt to manage variables that might disrupt the organization and they provide reassurance in the form of orderly charts and rules that paint a neat picture of a world that can be controlled by the right people applying the right pressure.

As we evaluate the usefulness of the machine model of church organization for a new age, we must ask whether those predictions and promises are borne out by reality, or whether they are merely illusions of control. Does life inevitably work toward decline and death, or does it naturally move toward more abundant life? Do things always go as planned? Is it right – ethically or theologically – to assume that people are like machine parts? What about their gifts, their passions, and their creativity to respond uniquely to the particular circumstances and challenges they encounter in their ministry? And where is God in all of it? Machine models neither invite nor welcome any of those seemingly valuable assets because they introduce variability and disrupt the way things are and need to stay. But at what cost do we ignore the full potential of God's good creation?

Looking back on the machine model era of organizational life, Wheatley notes that, "When we conceived of ourselves as machines, we gave up most of what is essential to being human. We created ourselves devoid of spirit, will, passion, compassion, emotions, even intelligence. Machines have none of these characteristics innately, and none of them can be built into its specifications" (Finding 19). Under the sway of machine model assumptions, "We have reduced and described and separated things into cause and effect, and drawn the world in lines and boxes" (Wheatley Leadership 29). We have lived with the belief that, through science and reason, "we would figure everything out. We would control it all, even life and death" so that somewhere along the way, "science displaced God" (Leadership 31).

No doubt science does provide a foundation for much of our understanding of the world. That is not necessarily a problem. But which science? While the living systems paradigm is gaining prominence with support from scientists working in specialties like quantum physics, chaos theory, and network theory, and though it lies at the core of pioneering approaches to organizational life advocated by experts like Wheatley and many others, it is not yet universally embraced. Instead we are in a transitional place that feels much like the leading edge of a weather front where the atmosphere is quite unsettled and sometimes pretty stormy.

For now, we can mark where we are in the transition from one organizational worldview to another. For example, you have bumped up against the limits of the machine paradigm and wandered into the realm of living systems if you have ever wondered why it's so hard to get people to do what you want them to do; people generally can't be made to do what they don't want to do. You have flirted with the boundary between the paradigms if you have ever sought to understand why some very successful activities, programs and ministries seem to just pop up out of nowhere while others that receive extensive planning and support fail to yield anything like the hoped-for results; life is not simply a matter of command and control in which even the best laid plans easily translate into realities. You are straddling the paradigms if you believe there must be a better way for your church to organize to do its work, one that frees creative energy and stirs new ideas, one that might even involve discovering God in some new way. Perhaps, whether you know it or not, you are hoping for the full emergence of a new paradigm. Its time could be right now.

3) LOOKING AROUND: GENERATIONAL INFLUENCES ON CHURCH ORGANIZATION

It's the middle of the week at a mid-sized church in a mid-sized town in the middle of America. One by one, members of the church board gather for their monthly meeting. The first to arrive is Cindy, a 60 year old accountant who is still nursing injuries to the arm that was twisted to get her to serve as board president for another year. She is followed closely by Laura, 48, the pastor who is in her seventh year with this, her first congregation. She enters the room with the ministerial intern, Mike, who, at 25 years of age, is one of a now-rare breed of students pursuing ministry as a first career. Bob, a 52 year old lawyer arrives next, straight from the office and looking for a snack. Fifty year old Brenda arrives, relieved to be done grading the stack of papers for the class she teaches at the community college. Pleasant greetings are exchanged as the group welcomes Fred, the senior member at 79, a still-part-time mechanic, and Marge, the 55 year old owner of the arts and crafts store on Main Street. They are followed closely by 49 year-old Lori, the nurse at the local elementary school, and George, the 65 year old CEO of the biggest bank in town. Eighteen-year-old Kevin enters next, the designated youth representative who is elated to get a break from college applications and financial aid forms. Forty-five year old corporate executive Jane rushes in, apologizing for being late because her baby-sitter got held up in traffic. A seventy year old retired marine, Jerry, enters the board room and takes his usual seat. Debbie, 57, enters as well, after a long day of work on her farm. Just as the meeting is being called to order, Henry, a 56 year old high school teacher, settles into the last seat left at the table.

Made up of many more people representing older generations than younger, this church board could represent many if not most Mainline church boards these days.

Generational differences can influence the ways individuals approach organizations. Assuming that each generation has experienced the world differently and that each has, in fact, experienced a different world, we can benefit from exploring some of the generational deposits in the geological make-up of our congregations. Appreciating generational differences can promote a level of cross-generational empathy that can diffuse interpersonal tensions, enrich conversation, and deepen collaboration. Such exploration reinforces the importance of reaching out to and including people in every phase of life.

Generational cohorts tend to be rather cohesive groups because of common experiences that lead to shared values about such things as institutions and organizations. The world has been a different place for older members than it has been for younger ones, and each generation has been shaped in a way that is different from the generations before and after.

Professor Gary L. McIntosh, who has published widely on generational issues relative to the church, offers useful guidance when he writes that, "From early childhood each generation sees and interprets life events and experiences from within the context of the group. Over a period of time a particular generation becomes oriented to a particular way of thinking and perceiving. This process is called socialization" (One World 30). To varying degrees, each person embodies the experiences and values of their particular generational cohort.

While there are useful ways to think about generational factors in church life, it is important to keep in mind that there are no hard and fast rules that permit sweeping assumptions about how individuals, regardless of their generation, approach organizational life. The risk of making such assumptions is highlighted in the story of a local congregation that was working through a process to decide whether they would declare themselves to be Open and Affirming for gay, lesbian, bisexual, and transgender people. There was initial speculation that the older generations would be resistant while younger generations would be more open to the idea. However, it turned out that the congregation's most senior members were largely supportive and even encouraging about Open and Affirming while some middle-aged members were deeply troubled by the prospect.

With that cautionary word in mind, a brief glimpse into the socializing experiences of each of the five generations now represented in our congregations can help us think through some of the ways generational differences might influence peoples' approaches to organizational life, highlighting possible generationally-derived expectations and needs, and illuminating generational values that might shape decision-making.[1]

The GI Generation

Born before 1928, the group that has been referred to as the "Greatest Generation" (Pew Millennial Study) or the GI Generation is the most senior generation alive today. The youngest of them are now 86 years old. During their formative years, automobiles were still a relatively new addition to daily life and airplane flight was still in its infancy. A world war had just ended and the United States was on the side of victory in global conflict. Times were generally good and the cultural and economic prosperity of the Roaring Twenties included a migration toward cities and the granting of voting rights to women. The bold and expansive spirit of the age was captured in Lindberg's flight across the Atlantic Ocean, even as tight-knit communities tended to anchor individuals and families in close proximity to each other. With the close of the 1920's, members of this generation were suddenly confronted with a massive financial downturn before they went off to win another world war.

Churches often grew in neighborhoods from which they also tended to draw their members, and it was not unusual for particular families to dominate church leadership

---

[1] There is no definitive categorization of generations. Information upon which this section is based was culled from a wide variety of sources, including Roof (Spiritual Marketplace), McIntosh (One World), Pew Research, and multiple internet sources.

across generations. Neighborhood churches, often organized around specific languages and cultures, generated tremendous loyalty and encouraged personal ownership of congregations, their ministries, and their futures.

The Builder Generation

The Builder generation was born between 1928 and 1945, and they are currently between 85 and 69 years of age. The Builders learned frugality and the value of stability in the midst of crises and challenges that dominated their formative years. The oldest members of this generation were born as the Roaring Twenties abruptly gave way to the Great Depression which, despite recent events, remains the most significant financial downturn in American history. People worked hard though paid work was hard to find. Large government programs literally saved people who were otherwise barely clinging to life. The Depression was followed by World War II which cost tens of millions of lives around the world, including hundreds of thousands of American lives, and reshaped world politics for decades to come.

The war effort that consumed this nation reinforced the importance of clear lines of accountability and military efficiency in a well-ordered society. After all, that order and discipline had seen people through great trial and tribulation and made it possible for them to emerge triumphant on the other side. Social boundaries and roles were very clear, and family, church, and country were especially important. By unifying around a core national identity and building stable institutions to support it, this generation weathered storm after storm. Members of this generation were the driving force behind the heyday of large institutions and the surging popularity of churches and community organizations in the 1950's and 1960's.

Builders have watched with care and concern as the Mainline churches they expanded to serve booming congregations now increasingly appear to be on the verge of bust. Yet despite increasing concerns about personal mobility and other pragmatic issues, members of this generation still tend to show up in church as often as they can, often occupying the same pews that have been theirs for decades. They possess the long-view of modern history. What will be preserved of their generation's great institutional legacy? Will their work crumble like the bricks and mortar of now-ancient church buildings that dot the American landscape?

The Boomer Generation

The largest generation in American history is referred to as the Baby Boom or Boomer Generation and was born between 1946 and 1964. By their sheer numbers, they have had and continue to exert tremendous influence over American culture and institutional life. Boomers are now between 68 and 50 years old. By and large, they grew up in stable families. Dan R. Dick in *Bursting the Bubble*, describes the Boomer experience this way: "We were 4H'd, Scouted, Junior Achieved, sock-hopped, prommed, jocked, cheerled, and performing-arted like never before" (11). But while their parents valued stability, loyalty, and order, Boomers powered a massive pendulum swing in the other direction. As a group, Boomers pushed back hard against all that their parents stood for. The pushback was significant enough to warrant a label – the Generation Gap – that awakened social scientists to generational differences in the first place.

Increasingly rebellious and suspicious of institutions, Boomers challenged leaders and embraced "causes" for the greater good. Wade Clark Roof, in his seminal study *Spiritual Marketplace*, writes that, "For the boomer generation trust in institutions has been, and continues to be, a vexing and unresolved matter" (47). They lived through the "Cold War" and were caught up in battles over civil rights and women's rights, started a sexual revolution, witnessed the assassinations of important cultural icons, watched a presidency collapse under the weight of public scrutiny, and saw the eventual end of a horribly divisive war.

Despite their early emphasis on larger issues, Boomers have also valued personal satisfaction and prosperity. They are a generation of "spiritual seekers" (Roof) who have been selective in terms of church affiliation, if they affiliate at all. Their consumer-driven approach to religion has spawned a movement of seeker-oriented churches and megachurches that have abandoned traditional ways of being church for more contemporary alternatives. Will Boomers' efforts to make the world a better place really amount to anything in the end, or will they go up in a puff of smoke?

The Buster Generation

The "Busters" of Generation X were born between 1965 and 1980, making them now between 49 and 34 years of age. Probably the most misunderstood and perhaps the least-appreciated generation, they were initially referred to as "slackers." They have come of age as personal computers became available and then became ubiquitous. Newspapers and magazines that were so important to previous generations have largely been replaced in their lifetimes by a plethora of online resources. Busters have witnessed the end of the Cold War that had been such a defining factor for previous generations, and they have lived with the looming threat of attacks by international and homegrown terrorists. They have watched as the economy became global and the world became a village. Increased mobility and flexibility have made it easier than ever to travel the country and the world while still being virtually connected to family and friends.

In general, boundaries have become less clear and less important to members of this generation whose families have not necessarily followed traditional models — remember that Boomers are their parents. They have lived in a world of diversity on many key dimensions, and are generally accepting of change, even if they tend to be skeptical about where it might lead. Busters have not necessarily rebelled against church as much as they were not, by and large, acculturated into it in the same way earlier generations were.

The Bridger Generation

Though information about Bridgers, who are also known as Generation Y or the Millennial Generation, is just starting to emerge, this cohort is receiving considerable attention from those who study generational differences. And they are particularly worthy of our attention since they will be the bearers of the church's most distant foreseeable future. They were born after 1981 and are all now younger than 33 years old. They have captured the interest of people who study generational issues in that "the cohort born between 1990 and 2000 is the largest in 30 years" (Rasmus 11).

Their world is the world we are all living in, profoundly pluralistic, inextricably interdependent, yet increasingly polarized. Terrorism is a real and present danger that has colored their world, especially since September 11, 2001. Bridger families come in all shapes and sizes with variable expectations regarding roles relative to gender or other factors. Theirs is a hyper-aware world in which information is instantly available, from nearly anywhere, about nearly anything. Advances in technology hold great promise and happen faster and faster every day. Meaning-making is complicated by levels of intricacy unimagined by older generations. There is even an emerging body of neurological evidence suggesting that the brains of younger generations, immersed as they are in technology, multi-tasking and the challenges of contemporary society, are appreciably different than the brains of older generations.

A recent Pew Research Center study ("Religion Among the Millennials") suggests that Bridgers are significantly less affiliated with religious organizations than any previous generation, continuing a trend that began decades ago. The same study finds that, while a smaller percentage of Bridgers believe in the absolute existence of God compared to older generations, still over half say they do indeed believe in God's existence. There are questions about whether and how Bridgers will relate to churches as institutions, and about what kind of "church" might be most engaging for them.

Shifts in Worldview

Underlying that flow from one generation to the next was a fundamental change in worldview that phased in along the way. GI's, Builders and Boomers have lived mostly in a world dominated by modernism while Busters and Bridgers were born into a world that has become increasingly postmodern. We will explore modernism and postmodernism in more detail in the next reflection.

Even as you are examining the way your church is organized to do its work, you might find yourself and your congregation flummoxed by intergenerational tensions. This reflection gives you a starting point for recognizing, naming, and understanding those tensions. People engaged in cross-generational conversation will benefit from approaching generational differences with respect and an open mind, listening to hear people's connections with their own generational experiences while working to prepare the church for the generations that are coming.

QUESTION FOR REFLECTION: How has growing up in your generation shaped who you are and what you believe about churches and institutions?

A seminary friend had a bumper sticker that asked "Where are we going and why am I in this hand-basket?" The question implies a foreboding sense of doom. I wonder how many people in Mainline churches are feeling a bit of that same sense these days as they think about the present and future of their congregations and the larger denominational bodies of which they are a part.

Decades of Decline

Since the peak of church involvement in the United States in the 1950's and 60's, Mainline churches have experienced dramatic declines in membership, attendance, and financial giving. In some cases the losses seem overwhelming. For example, in 2009, the *National Council of Churches Yearbook* reported that the United Church of Christ underwent a 6.01 percent drop in membership from the previous year. While that decline was higher than other denominational groups for that year, all Mainline churches experienced yet another year of continued numerical decline. According to the *Presbyterian Outlook* (August 18, 2010), the Presbyterian Church (USA) in 2008 experienced its steepest membership loss since reunion in 1983, losing nearly 70,000 members.

United Methodist Bishop Robert Schnase notes that one United Methodist Conference was deemed to be "'average' among mainline judicatories" even though it lost eighty-five thousand members and two hundred churches in forty years and witnessed an increase in the median age of current members to fifty-eight (In Rendle ix).

A report by the Association of Religion Data Archives reviewed data from the 2010 census which shows an average 12.8 percent decline among Catholic and Mainline Protestant denominations during the ten-year period since the previous census. The United Church of Christ led the field with losses nearly double the average. Among Protestant churches, only Southern Baptists experienced a miniscule increase of 0.1

percent. Yet simply keeping pace with population growth during that same period would have required growth of 9.7 percent. Interestingly, during that same ten-year span, Unitarian Universalists, long known for their open theological stance and intense commitment to social justice, experienced a national increase of 15.8 percent with individual state results as dramatic as 42 percent.

In 2012, the Pew Research Center reported that, for the first time in history, the number of people who consider themselves "unaffiliated" with a religious community rose above 20 percent, fully one fifth of the population of the United States. For people younger than thirty years of age, the "unaffiliated" number climbed to one-third, pointing toward a continuation of existing trends. Called "nones" because they listed no church affiliation, the group is made up of relatively small proportions of atheists and agnostics (six percent of the total population) along with a larger proportion of people who simply do not participate in corporate religion (14 percent of the total population).

In fact, if your church is like most Mainline churches, you need only look around on Sunday morning to validate the reality that the church is not what it used to be. One middle-aged woman reported looking out one Sunday morning at people gathered for worship in the church of which she was a lifelong member. With a sense of surprise bordering on utter shock she reported that her immediate reaction was, "God, we've gotten old!" She recalled the days when the church was brimming with activity, when young children played in the pulpit and hid in the choir loft after worship, when classrooms were crowded to overflowing during Sunday School while the youth group met regularly every week – and there were actually enough youth to call it a group. She longed for the days when every generation was well-represented among the church's numbers.

Of course the declining numbers have led some to speculate about the future of the church in general. Articles and books have been written with titles like John Cobb's "Do Oldline Churches Have a Future?" and Robert D. Schieler's

Revive Your Mainline Congregation: Prescriptions for Vital Church Life. The cover of the latter features what appear to be waves like you'd find on an echocardiogram. Lifting statistics from an organization called empty tomb, inc., Schieler writes that, "unless mainline Protestant churches do things significantly differently than over the past thirty-five to fifty years, most United Church of Christ congregations (my denomination, for example) will be gone by 2032" (9, parentheses his). There are numerous other books and articles that strike similar tones.

Paul Nixon, in *I Refuse to Lead a Dying Church*, claims that "most of the denominational faith communities that first evangelized North America are now rapidly down shifting toward oblivion and near extinction" (9). He further makes these assertions: "Most mainline pastors are leading churches that will not exist by the year 2100; many of these churches will be gone long before that. More than half of the congregations that call themselves United Methodist, Evangelical Lutheran, Presbyterian, Episcopal, Disciples of Christ, American Baptist, and United Church of Christ will likely disappear sometime in the next half century. Thousands of future pastors currently training in university divinity schools will soon graduate with a zest for ministry, only to find themselves deployed to do deathbed vigil somewhere – tending a rapidly aging congregation that has little energy to do what's necessary to thrive" (9). What a powerful, earth-shaking image!

Even Richard Ogle, writing from outside the church, chimes in: "Plenty of hubs are massively interlinked to other hubs and nodes, but aren't particularly dynamic: mainstream Protestantism, for instance…" (252). The implication is that connections exist linking to and from Mainline Protestant churches, but they are not heavily trafficked.

It would seem that a case could be made, based on available statistics and current predictions, that the church will soon cease to exist as we know it. On one hand, that fate, accompanied as it is by undertones of despair, justifiably strikes fear in the hearts of good and faithful people. On the other hand, however, one could argue – as I do as a central point of this book – that the church ceasing to exist as we know it is precisely the way forward. In fact it may be so that the only way forward is letting go of what the church has been for the sake of what the church can be now and what it will need to be for the foreseeable future.

Letting go need not be a reason for alarm but a hopeful and necessary next step toward a new church for a new day. We've all likely heard stories about people emerging from near-death experiences with a new appreciation for life. Wheatley offers this perspective: "Accepting death, far ahead of its appearance, is richly liberating. Suddenly we find courage, energy, determination and levels of freedom never available when we were crouched down in self-protection. Accepting death opens us, frees us, clarifies life, simplifies decisions" (Perseverance 91). Randy Pausch, in his now famous The Last Lecture, certainly affirmed life even in the face of his own imminent death. More recently, a young man named Zach Sobiech made a song called "Clouds" for which the video went viral. Just weeks from his death, he gave the world an opportunity to think again about life.

Wheatley would help us here to understand that churches, as all living systems, are dissipative structures. "They dissipate or give up their form in order to recreate themselves into new forms" (Leadership 80). Dissipation, giving up one form, becomes the foundation and creates the need for self-organization, which is how systems evolve and thrive. That same dynamic is, of course, important to Christian theology which emphasizes self denial and self surrender, and revolves around the model of Jesus' death as the way to new life.

Embracing Change

But rather than simply abandoning what we know for the sake of what is still in many ways unknowable, we can benefit from understanding what we can about the world for which we need to reorganize. It may be worth stating the obvious here: the world of the earliest Christian church was fundamentally different than the world of the Protestant Reformation, for example, which was fundamentally different than the world of the American Revolution which was fundamentally different than the world of 1960's America which was fundamentally different than the world in which we find ourselves right now. In each of those eras, the church became what it needed to be for the times.

Based on that pattern, we are probably safe to go the additional step of recognizing that the world of tomorrow will be fundamentally different than the world of today. Think about it. We are living in a new world and, in a very real sense, the world gets newer every day. Each day brings new challenges and choices even as it brings brand new possibilities. This is a time when, as Roof notes, "Old certainties collapse as new mysteries arise" (8). Rather than thinking about the church still being here *despite* all the change that is occurring – as if the main task is to navigate a mine field or survive a battle of attrition, might we more productively and hopefully think about the church still being here *because* of all that change? Change is not an obstacle to be overcome but an invitation to be accepted to move forward based on the new circumstances and conditions that characterize the world into which we are now living.

At a most fundamental level, making the transition from what has been to what will be requires that churches abandon their machine model fears of inevitable decline as a terminal prognosis. Instead, churches are invited to embrace change as a way of bringing to life the unlimited possibilities inherent in all living systems.

An Age of Posts

If the journey forward starts with understanding where we are, where are we? What can we say about the world in which we live? We can begin by understanding that we live in what has been called the "age of posts." Jim Kitchens provides a wonderful analysis of three particular "posts" that can be only briefly touched upon here. He describes a world that is postmodern, post-Christian, and post-denominational. He writes of each as a cultural wave and concludes that, "*all three* cultural waves are crashing onto the shore of congregational life at the same time, each magnifying the impact of the other two. We're not just looking at gentle waves lapping onto the shore, then. We're dealing with a tsunami!" (6). Yet there are ways to understand the awesome forces now bearing down. And knowing can help us resituate ourselves on higher ground.

Postmodern

First, we live in a postmodern world. This is in contrast to the "modern" era which began with the Enlightenment and found its stride in Newton's time. The shift between modernism and postmodernism, which began in art and architecture but gradually pervaded the culture, is profound. Modernism held that there was essentially one universal truth, and if we looked hard enough and brought the right resources to bear, we could and inevitably would discover it. There was a right answer for each of the big questions. Postmodernism, on the other hand, allows for the coexistence of multiple truths, dependent on one's perspective and a host of circumstances. Instead of right and wrong, postmodernism allows for right and right. If modernism was black and white, postmodernism illuminates shades of gray. If modernism pulled for uniformity and conformity, postmodernism invites and even encourages diversity and plurality. If modernism drew clear boundaries, postmodernism features lines that are blurred, permeable, fluid, or non-existent to begin with. With particular regard to organizational life, modernism called for hierarchical structures and lines of accountability, while postmodernism is less prescriptive and more malleable. And, like it or not, we live in a postmodern world.

Post-Christian

Second, we live in a post-Christian world, which describes the transition away from the time Christian churches were simply "the church." In the era of American Christendom (Robinson Transforming 3), Christianity was the *de facto* civil religion of America. Christian churches had special status in communities. Christian prayer was routinely said in schools. "Blue laws" limited commerce on Sundays, and the cultural expectation was that people would be in church then anyway. It was simply unheard of for soccer tournaments and dance competitions to be held on Sunday mornings.

Slowly, however, beginning in the late 1960's and since, that has changed. Christianity began to lose its special status as people wandered away from churches. Under the umbrella of spiritual seeking, some people gravitated toward other faith traditions that have presented appealing religious and spiritual alternatives. Others drifted away from church altogether or began to think of themselves as "spiritual but not religious," interested in God and general spirituality but not "church" *per se*.

In general, attending church at all is now one of the myriad activities from which people must choose. For many, weekends are a prime opportunity to get done what doesn't get done during the week, the routine stuff of life that is not as easily managed in families in which there is less likely to be a stay-at-home person during the week.

Anthony Robinson, in *Transforming Congregational Culture*, claims that "the 1960's and 70's saw a succession of events that tore holes in the sacred canopy of American society and its civil religion" (5). But the changes were not perceived until late in the process, or they were misunderstood. I remember growing up in Pittsburgh as the steel mills declined. Because steel had played such a vital role in the region's culture and economy, people were exceedingly slow to accept the possibility that the mills could or would close, despite ominous warning signs. As a result, people did little to prepare for what would be a horribly traumatic loss of life as they knew it. The church's response to the passing of the Era of Christendom has been similarly sluggish and slow. It conjures up images of flat-footedness and deer in headlights.

We get a glimpse into the gradual changes in church life that began decades ago in the 1967 publication entitled *The Church: Design for Survival*, by E. Glenn Hinson. His book begins, "These are disturbing days for the churches of America. Having become accustomed to almost uninterrupted growth, they now can see signs of approaching decline. Although still strong numerically and financially, they are beginning to experience a drop in attendance and a waning of enthusiasm among their members" (9). He goes on to ask, "Is this the beginning of a trend… Is it, hopefully, only a passing thing, like that witnessed now and again in Christian history?" It has surely become clearer over the intervening decades that the decline was not a "passing thing" at all.

The end of Christendom has a wide range of possible implications for the way we make decisions about many aspects of church life. For example, in my current church, weekly bulletin space is at a premium. Yet we reprint the Lord's Prayer every week. There was a time when we could assume that people knew the words. Now there are no guarantees. In general, post-Christendom summons churches to rethink church membership in a world in which people are less willing to pledge long-term institutional loyalty, volunteering in a world in which people's busy lives are already packed full with commitments, and stewardship in a world in which people's resources are already stretched thin.

Post-Denominational

Third, we live in a post-denominational world. As Christianity has fallen from its esteemed status in American culture, so has denominational loyalty been on the decline. There was a time when denominational affiliation was particularly meaningful, and it was accompanied by education in denominational history and polity. Commitment to particular denominations was assumed, through thick and thin, ups and downs, and all other circumstances. People were even willing to wait out pastors they were not especially fond of rather than affiliate with a neighboring church from another denomination.

Over time, however, those lines have blurred and loyalties have weakened. The gravitational pull of denominations is no longer as strong as it once was. This also traces back to the 1950's and 1960's when well-intentioned ecumenical efforts emphasized commonalities and collaboration between denominations. And with the cultural shift toward a consumer orientation, people have become more selective about churches based on many factors which may or may not include denominational connection. For many people, local congregations matter more than wider church ties. Factors such as geographic proximity, worship styles, specialized programs, and coffee hour snacks can play a larger role in people's decisions than denominational affiliation. At one point I remember seeing an insightful comic strip that showed two people sitting in front of a pastor's desk. The caption read something like "I think we'll go with the Unitarians. They have a gym."

Beyond those particular dimensions of postmodernism, post-Christendom and post-denominationalism, we are also challenged to continue coming to terms with what it means to live in what is ominously known as a "post-9/11 world."

In her book *The Practicing Congregation: Imagining a New Old Church*, Diana Butler Bass offers one more "post" that challenges some of the other assumptions. She states that we are in a *"post-*decline period" (11). In fact she believes that there are signs of stabilization and new life within American Protestantism that have yet to make their way into the narrative being told about churches in popular culture. She claims, "That is the *new* news: American Protestantism is changing – maybe more than it has in a century" (11). Throughout the remainder of the book and in her *Christianity for the Rest of Us*, she offers compelling evidence to support her conclusion.

Changing Times

There are other social and cultural factors that also warrant attention relative to church organization. Think, for example, about the changes that have taken place regarding the availability of information. Who'd have thought that esteemed encyclopedia companies would be effectively run out of business by information accessible at people's fingertips by way of the internet? "The quantity of information used to double about every fifty years; now information doubles every three years and soon will be down to eighteen months" (Patton 24). At what point will our capacity to keep pace with new information simply be exhausted? What does it mean for church organization that communication that used to take days, weeks, or months can now happen instantly around the world? What are the implications of now having hundreds of television and radios stations to choose from instead of three major networks and a smattering of local stations? Whether we are better or worse off than we used to be, we are challenged to come to terms with living in an increasingly complex world that offers only change as a constant.

Vital Choices

This is a challenging time for churches which now play a much different role in people's lives than they did when our current organizational structures flourished. People are bombarded by more scheduling choices than ever, church being but one of the competing organizations and interests vying for their time, energy, and resources. Different views have developed toward church membership, attendance, financial giving, and commitment to volunteer activities. Yet churches have an opportunity to adapt to changing circumstances by re-inventing church organization.

Kitchens is one voice among many calling for a paradigm shift that anticipates a future that is coming whether we are ready or not, and in important ways is already here. Rendle proclaims that we are now on a chaotic journey in the wilderness which requires a new response.

Wheatley surely expresses urgency to start thinking differently about the world and how we live in it. She notes that what had been her "voice of invitation needs to be prefaced by a clear, more insistent voice. Now I am the town crier sounding the alarm. The world has changed" (Leadership x).

This is in many ways a time of vital choices for churches, regarding church organization and all other aspects of church life. Widely respected United Methodist Bishop William H. Willimon declares that "Church as usual, ministry as we've always done it, just won't get the job done. We've got to realize that the ground beneath our feet has shifted and that the church is being given a new mission to a changed world. Start screaming" (in Kitchens viii).

QUESTION FOR REFLECTION: C. Kirk Hadaway offers this provocative and critical observation: "Mainline churches are designed to decline, not by driving people away, but by failing to be useful, relevant, or interesting" (27). In what ways might that be true? If it's true, how can it be otherwise?

_____

_____

5) ASSESSING THE WAY WE'VE ALWAYS DONE IT

Psychologist Abraham Maslow once said, "If all you've got is a hammer, you tend to treat everything like a nail." Churches and church leaders would be justified in asking, "Well, what else is there?" Granted, there are not a lot of viable organizational alternatives to the way we've always done it. This program is an attempt to fill that void and we will shortly turn to practical possibilities for what else churches might do. In this reflection, however, we continue our journey of discovery by attempting to understand where we are in terms of specific practices. If nothing else, this brief rehearsal of the way we've always done it will focus our attention on what we mostly take for granted about church life. Here we shall explore the ways church history, machine model organizational thinking, and generational differences come together in the form of practices that are common in churches today.

Organizationally, churches have drawn on all three sources to design sometimes-elaborate organizational charts with lines of accountability and responsibility drawn carefully between blocks and other blocks. Constitutions, bylaws, operating manuals and similar documents set forth what their authors believed ought to be done to deal with all matters great and small, from how the congregation makes decisions to where the filters are stored for Coffee Hour on Sunday morning. One answer is presented for situations in which many answers might be generated. There are even multiple books on the market that purport to list essentially everything you need to know about church administration, all laid out and ready to apply, and complete with a sample "Custodial Daily Work Checklist" (Powers 72). That is not the approach being advocated here.

Maybe you've heard the saying, "If you always do what you've always done, you'll always get what you've always got." In light of the changed and changing circumstances in which churches find themselves these days, staying the course likely means continuing a steady decline into eventual obsolescence. Of course Einstein reminds us that doing the same thing again and again and expecting a different result is the very definition of insanity.

Dan Hotchkiss, in his thorough book *Governance and Ministry* points out that, "many congregations organize the way they did in 1950, with boards and committees dutifully meeting, taking minutes, passing budgets, adopting or defeating motions. Each committee controls all work in its assigned sphere and has to do the work as well. New ideas require many conversations and approvals; old ideas escape serious evaluation. It is a system well designed to resist change, or – to put it differently – to preserve tradition" (19). The critique is not that such models of church organization were wrong in 1950, but that they can't reasonably be expected to work now in the context of a radically different world.

As we explore new ways of being church, it is entirely appropriate to remember that our forebears have handed down organizational structures and processes that have served congregations well for a long time. Indeed what we now have as a starting place are the best responses by people in past eras to build and maintain faithful church communities given the world in which they lived. They integrated cultural circumstances, prevailing worldviews, and practical solutions to create a way of organizing that indeed built extremely successful churches that have forever changed the course of American history. Our task is to do precisely what they did: to pioneer organizational models that work for the age in which we live.

With a true appreciation of the way churches have functioned, it is important that we also allow ourselves to take a critical look at organizational structures and dynamics that can no longer be expected to meet the needs of present and future generations. Such a critical look may well lead us to some difficult choices. Yet it is hard to conceive of a way that organizational innovation can happen in congregations without jettisoning ways of being and doing that no longer serve a useful purpose.

Before reviewing common organizational practices, it might be helpful to think about what church organization is not; it is not a vehicle for involving people in church life. Respected church consultant Kennon Callahan states clearly that "The purpose of the organizational structure in the local church is not to 'involve' people. Years ago, the myth was spawned that the way to involve people is to put them on a committee, and the results of that myth have been among the most harmful and destructive factors contributing to many congregations' status as declining or dying churches" (59). People don't come to church to be on a committee. They may come to find social interaction or safe harbor in a storm. They may come so that they and their children can receive theological education and spiritual formation. They may come seeking some larger sense of meaning or for a whole host of other reasons. But it is probably safe to say that a little suspicion is appropriate if someone identifies a desire for committee membership as one of their top reasons for joining a church.

Church Structures

Let's think about church structures. Though every congregation is organized differently, there are probably common structures that are worth reflecting on here.

Organizational charts, whether formal or informal, attempt to map out organizations by assigning each individual or group a block (or circle or other geometric figure) that is set out in relation to other blocks according to hierarchical ranking and functional emphasis. The result is typically some sort of pyramid shape. The most powerful blocks, containing fewer people, are placed on the top of the chart and the least powerful blocks, which include the most people, are placed near the bottom, usually clustered with other blocks that are similar in some meaningful way. All blocks are nameless, faceless. Depending on the size and sophistication of the organization, there can be multiple middle levels built into the chart as well. More complex charts include lines connecting blocks in ways that indicate accountability so that it becomes possible to trace which group is accountable to which other groups all the way to the top of the pyramid where all responsibility ultimately rests.

The operational assumption is that groups and individuals represented by blocks that are placed highest on the chart are responsible for making significant decisions, approving large financial expenditures, serving as final arbiters of conflict, and generally maintaining equilibrium in the system. Simultaneously, they are uniquely charged with and expected to provide leadership and bring about necessary change and thus straddle the perilous fault line between constancy and change. Accordingly, people occupying lower spots in the pyramid are typically conditioned to look to those at the top to meet the needs of the system, even by anticipating potential issues and difficulties and providing answers for vexing problems. In so doing, those lower on the chart relegate themselves to subordinate roles from which they can largely absolve themselves of much real responsibility.

When they do come up with new ideas, those occupying positions near the top of the chart typically push them down through the system according to already-established lines of accountability and responsibility. That means of conveying ideas based on authority that runs from top to bottom in organizations is commonly referred to as "command and control leadership" which accurately evokes images of military leadership.

Church organizational structures can become quite complicated, exhaustive, and exhausting. Hadaway offers the reminder that as a general rule, "Whether through planning or gathering 'ministry moss,' the organizational structure of the church tends to become more and more complex, overburdened, and unwieldy" (23). There is always the risk of building bureaucracy on top of bureaucracy in futile attempts to solve problems or cope with new realities.

Reflecting on elaborate and highly-regulated organizational structures, Tim Brown, the CEO of innovation firm IDEO, promises that "regulation-sized spaces tend to produce regulation-sized ideas" (36). Contrasting traditional, machine-model organizational structures with organization from a living systems perspective, Wheatley warns quite ominously that "Organizations held at equilibrium by well-designed organizational charts die. In self-organizing systems, people need access to everyone; they need to be free to reach anywhere in the organization to accomplish work" (Finding 40). In tightly-structured systems, that kind of access can be extremely limited. Have you ever been in a situation in your church where following "official channels" required that you talk to one person in one part of the organization to communicate with another person in another part of the organization? Maybe you have used language like "going up the ladder" or following the "chain of command."

Committees are almost always included in church organizational schemes. Often the designated committees focus on particular aspects of church life that have been deemed in some way essential. Sometimes the longevity of committees is based on no more than that they have been around for as long as anyone can remember. Each committee is assigned a specific domain in which they function according to established bylaws or policies and procedures and each ultimately functions under the auspices of the church board.

To do their work, committees have meetings which tend to be regularly scheduled at pre-determined time intervals. Meetings typically follow "agendas" developed by those in leadership positions, typically called "chairpersons," most often based on a pre-established order which can include various sub-committee reports that tend to be more geared toward managing what is already happening than imagining anything new. In more formal committees, proceedings are recorded by a designated "secretary" in "minutes" which are typically made available for public review once they are approved.

In general, one might wonder how well churches can be propelled into the future by groups that are referred to as "standing committees" which are ironically under the direction of persons called "chairs."

Wheatley writes of the drudgery of meetings. She notes, "I have been here thousands of times before, literally. I am in a meeting... I am weary of the lists we make, the time projections we spin out, the breaking down and putting back together of problems. It does not work. The lists and charts do not capture experience. They only tell of our desire to control a reality that is slippery and evasive and perplexing beyond comprehension. Like bewildered shamans, we perform rituals passed down to us, hoping they will perform miracles" (Leading 28). Most often, they do not, despite our persistence.

With the expectation that each committee be staffed by a certain number of people for defined terms of multiple years, it does not take long for there to be more positions to fill than there are people willing to serve. At that point it is easy to slip into the mode of maintaining the organizational structure for its own sake, filling "slots" because they exist without really asking why they exist or what difference they make. At such times, there is high risk of the qualifications to fill the position becoming disconnected from any sense of appropriate fit between candidate and position, and of criteria being modified to include such minimal standards as breathing and being willing to be convinced to serve, or simply being too slow to get away.

Hadaway points out the risk that "We create organizational structure and delude ourselves into thinking that we are accomplishing something" (23). Sometimes, organizational charts and committee structures can be things of great beauty. But they are at best a means to ministry, not ministry itself.

Church Processes and Procedures

Just as organizational structures deserve a second look, so do the processes that drive what organizations do and determine how they do it.

At one point I had the opportunity to be part of a bylaws revision process in a local congregation. The committee set out to read through seventeen pages of bylaws, page-by-page, word-for-word. As it turned out, neither the church board that delegated the task nor the task force that accepted the charge had a clue as to the difficulty of the endeavor. Think about reading words formed into carefully-crafted articles that at some point in the document's revision process made perfect sense to some presumably wise person. Working with an existing document created what seemed to be a totally understandable temptation to drill down deeper, to close loopholes, tighten language, complete sequences, add more safeguards. All of that involved more writing not less. But here we had this already-unwieldy document that was rarely used and routinely ignored because of its complexity.

That temptation to over-regulate and over-write is very real, especially as congregations strive to manage anxiety and fear that accompany increased diversity and diminished resources in a world where answers are less clear than they used to be.

Perhaps in the spirit of being "people of the book," we know, for example, that denominations have grown what used to be pocket-sized books of order into "hefty tomes" that are now "far more regulatory than principled" (Kitchens 88). Congregations may be tempted as well to resolve matters of basic trust with prescriptive solutions and detailed regulations that are dutifully written down and carefully added to ever-expanding three-ring notebooks that ultimately gather dust on an office bookshelf.

It is worth asking whether having things written down ensures that they are going to happen or whether written documents create an illusion of control that is harmfully deceptive in the long-run. Does your experience bear out a connection between what is planned, written, or regulated and what actually happens in real-life? Have you ever had a sign-up sheet where someone signed up to do something and then did not show up? If you hand people a set of elaborate instructions, how much would you be willing to bet they will carry out the instructions as written?

A leadership team attempted to update its church's procedures manual in light of obvious and well-known differences between what was written for most committees and how the work of the committees had evolved since the manual was published approximately fifteen years earlier. So the leadership team asked each chairperson to submit an up-to-date description of their committee's present operations. Quite surprisingly, the returned documents contained a couple of wording changes, but none of them addressed any substantive changes whatsoever! There was a nearly complete disconnect between what was written and what was really happening. People were quite willing to ignore the process of writing things down in the interest of actually doing the work. It wasn't that the groups and committees weren't doing wonderful things – they were indeed. Just not in the way that was prescribed by people writing in a different time under different circumstances.

Not only does writing things down not necessarily change what really happens, but each rule and regulation, each policy and procedure can become like yet another arrow shot by the Lilliputians strapping Gulliver to the ground. And each has the potential of limiting God's free movement throughout the congregation and the world.

Over-writing, over-prescribing, and over-regulating also run the risk of shifting the basic dynamic of church life. They set the stage for the work of the church being done by some version of an impersonal administrative unit far away from where the action is – and quite remote from where ministry occurs. Doing so reinforces the short-sighted notion of trickle down ministry and can squelch any flow of ideas from the people who are actively engaged in the church's work. In congregations that have no talent, imagination, or passion, that might be just fine. I'm guessing your congregation does indeed have talented, imaginative, and passionate people with ideas they're just waiting to share. What happens to the ideas that emerge as people live their lives and strive to fulfill their individual ministries? Where do ideas go once they bubble up? Do they burst when they come into contact with ideas that are trickling down?

Rendle (p. 70) writes that "the impulse to control through requirements does not result in clarity and tidiness but in fact creates complexity that further constrains and inhibits movement and change" (70). Donald R. Keough, former president of Coca Cola, adds his perception that "the geometrically elegant machinery of the organization should not get in the way of the human creativity and productivity of individuals" (118). Nor, I would add, should it be permitted to impede or otherwise limit the workings of the Spirit.

Too much organizational structure and too many rules and regulations can overwhelm people intending to engage in active ministry who are often left wondering whether they are doing things "right." And they can detract and distract from real mission and discipleship. Instead of inviting people to use the system to work toward fulfilling their aspirations to do good things, overdone church organization can turn the institution into nothing more than a scary monster that chases after people, gobbles them up, drains them of life, and dumps them off, depleted and defeated, on the other side. It would seem that churches might want to be different than that.

A Little Something Extra: Reflections on Robert's Rules of Order

Because they are interwoven into so much of church life, congregational conversation, and collective decision-making, Robert's Rules of Order deserve a special mention in this section on the way we've always done it. Written by General Henry Martyn Roberts in 1876 when he was called to preside over a community meeting, Robert's Rules have become the dominant way most organizations conduct formal business and make decisions. Congregations almost reflexively fall back on motions, seconds, and up and down votes, so much so that it is tremendously difficult for some to imagine that there could be another way. However, there are other ways that are worth considering and adopting. Honest, open, heart-to-heart conversation that works toward common ground and consensus, for example, is an effective alternative to parliamentary procedure.

Though widely used, Robert's Rules present their own problems. Kitchens writes that "the parliamentary procedure set out in Robert's Rules assumes an *adversarial* relationship between the parties seeking to come to a decision. It also favors the energetic extroverts in the room and tends to leave the insights of quieter and more introverted individuals out of the debate" (89). Of course operating under Robert's Rules ostensibly ensures that the voice of the minority is heard, but labeling minority and majority itself sets up an unbalanced relationship from the outset.

Rendle notes that, "With norms of agreement and pseudocommunity, people either avoid decisions altogether or use known tools such as Robert's Rules of Order to quickly measure where the majority stands and then impose agreement by expecting minority voices to shift and stand with the majority. The price paid for such harmony is the absence of new learning and denial of change" (124). There is the risk that Robert's Rules will be used to avoid taking on the greater challenge of having meaningful dialogue, and that new opportunities for learning and cohesion will be missed.

Charles M. Olsen, who presents a wide array of thoughtful approaches to church board interaction and decision-making, offers this sharp critique: "Robert's Rules of Order may protect us from one another. Yet I have observed that people use the 'Rules' to get their own needs met – to have fights, display their knowledge, massage their egos, vent their anger, test their opinions, punish their opponents, cover their fears, and hide from anything personal" (94). Importantly, he continues, "The parliamentary method assumes that no community base exists from which to interact and decide." It would seem that in churches, there is reasonable hope that that community base does indeed exist to open up other options.

Robert's Rules, especially in their full form which encompasses nearly all aspects of organizational life, can contribute to a scenario in which those who know the rules win the game, while people who don't know the rules end up repressing opinions and ideas or missing opportunities to express them. As such, the use of Robert's Rules can result in injustice and inequity.

Dan Hotchkiss (3) points out simply that the world is different than when Robert's Rules were written. We do well to account for changes in the world that have impact on congregational interactions. Surely, meaningful conversation is a mediating factor that can change the ways we interact, help deepen understanding, and build community. (A later reflection focuses on conversation and ways of making it work.)

QUESTION FOR REFLECTION: Does working within the organizational structures and processes of your congregation make you feel more like you are sprinting down an open track, needlessly trudging through a deep pool of water, or hopelessly sinking in quick sand?

SECTION TWO: EXPLORING A WORLD OF IDEAS

Having taken the opportunity to delve into some of the factors that have shaped current models of church organization and explored some of the current realities exerting impact on churches, we now turn our attention to alternative ways for congregations to function. In the next section of reflections, we will hear from Richard Ogle who will introduce us to a way of thinking that seeks to bring seemingly disparate ideas together to yield what he calls breakthrough creativity. Then we will hear from prominent voices in three seemingly disparate fields, living systems theory, design thinking, and Christian theology. Along the way, we will highlight useful ideas about how to reinvent church organization. But first, we will spend a moment reorienting ourselves in anticipation of bold new things.

6) REORIENTING

There are times when it feels like the pace of change is overwhelming. Perhaps sometimes it really is too much. We need not look far for proof. We can look to the way things have changed since we were each born, or since last year or last month or last week. Richard Ogle writes that, "Ours is an era when the future seems to be coming at us faster than ever, even as it becomes more complex and harder to understand" (24). And keeping up is hard to do.

Daft (26) notes that, "Today, almost all organizations operate in highly uncertain environments. Thus, we are involved in a significant period of transition, in which concepts of organization theory and design are changing as dramatically as they did with the dawning of the Industrial Revolution."

Kitchens observes about the Church in general that "our best efforts at ministry seem to be about a half-beat behind some new pulse that is beginning to course through the culture" (3). Similarly, Hadaway notes that "the future is a moving target. When we try to catch up with it, we find that we are always one step behind. When we try to anticipate its direction and arrive before it, we find that it has eluded us" (4). Doing what it's always done, and approaching organizational life as it always has, the Church in general just cannot seem to find a way to keep pace with the changes that surround it.

The obvious solution to the problem posed by lagging behind is to move faster. But I'm not sure moving fast is the church's best thing on any level, from universal to local. And I'm not sure it's about speed anyway. So what might be the matter?

What Is Church Organization?

We can work toward an answer to the question of what might be the matter by understanding what church organization is. In a very general sense, church organization refers to the way a church does what it does. A bit more specifically, church organization might be thought of as the ordering structures and processes by means of which a congregation accomplishes what it deems important, either explicitly or implicitly, at a given moment. For now, simply notice a few things about that definition. First, it refers to "ordering" as an inherent part of how the world works, rather than other seemingly related notions like managing, administering, or governing that are often assumed to be the primary focus of church organization. The latter terms imply imposition of control by a person or group in authority while the former recognizes that order may also emerge beyond the reach of any specific means or mechanisms of control. Second, it recognizes that what churches deem important is in fact important. And third, it focuses on a particular moment and allows for differences over time.

The bottom line is that church organization affects each and every aspect of church life in one way or another, directly or indirectly, constructively or deleteriously. Yet it is easy to take for granted the way churches are organized, to simply accept the way things are as the way they always have been and always will be, world without end. Amen?

Besides, talking about church organization lacks the glamour and glitz of presentations on the latest worship fads that have people trampling well-worn paths to the really big and seemingly still-growing churches. The relevance of church organization can easily be discounted relative to mission trips and community ministries which, it seems, rightfully stir feelings of authentic discipleship. Church organization can be the farthest thing from anyone's mind as they comfort a grieving family, or baptize a baby, or bless a new couple's union. And who really appreciates the importance of church organization when compared to lofty spiritual practices capable of drawing people closer to God? Isn't that, after all, what churches are supposed to do?

It would seem so. And church organization provides the foundation for all of those activities and for everything else a church does. At the end of the day, all of those ministry activities emerge from, depend on, and are accounted for according to the way congregations are organized. So optimizing church organization can make the difference between congregational life and death.

QUESTION FOR REFLECTION: What in your church is not in one way or another affected by the way your church is organized?

Anticipation

As Christians, we know about anticipatory waiting. Each year we lead into Christmas with Advent and Easter with Lent. Indeed, according to common views of salvation history, we are ultimately in a period of waiting and anticipation that we reaffirm every time we proclaim that "Christ has died. Christ is risen. Christ will come again."

We are now also in another kind of waiting, for the emergence of a new way for churches to organize to do their work. How might we approach this waiting period? How can we lean forward and make the most of this time in-between?

Toy Story Mania is one of the most popular attractions now at Walt Disney World. The attraction itself is a marvelous experience of full immersion in a thrilling, life-sized, interactive video game. But even getting there is part of the excitement. While lines are almost always long, the physical setting itself engages guests in a land of over-sized toys, games and imaginative murals. Complete with a lively Mr. Potato Head singing songs and posing for pictures, the queue is not just for fun. It helps people get into the spirit of the attraction and entices them onward. As legendary Disney designer John Hench writes, such experiences invite people to "play in the story environment" (5) even as they help them prepare for what might be coming.

In a similar way, I'd like to invite you to a spirit of playfulness as we begin to imagine a different world that our time together might lead us to. Let's get ourselves ready to experience other ways to be church, ways that encourage us to be our most creative selves as we respond to God's call and attend to the urgings of the Spirit.

Here are some ideas about how to get ready:

Be curious. In a world that is constantly changing, it is tempting and even deceptively comforting to think that we already know everything we need to know. If you do know all of the answers, I'd respectfully ask that you keep them to yourself for now. There is too much fun to be had by the rest of us as we peek around corners, look under rocks, and peer into the unknown. We may heed the advice of Jeffrey Goldstein in his wonderfully titled book *The Unshackled Organization* to "upset the apple-cart, uproot the roots, and rock the boat" (89). We might even choose what's behind "Door Number Two" just to see what's there. Rather than clinging to what we think we know, we might give ourselves permission to not know, and allow ourselves to be curious instead of certain. What will we discover that we'd never thought of before? Wheatley calls curiosity "the saving grace" (Leading 8). I wonder if that could be true for you and your congregation.

If we were to assume that we have all the answers, conversations would become less useful and even unnecessary, so interactions would be reduced to meaningless small-talk if they happen at all. Other people would be less valuable and their perspectives would be summarily rendered irrelevant, so community wouldn't matter. If we assume that we know it all, indeed even faith itself becomes something other than faith. Questions and curiosity, on the other hand, draw us into conversation and community where God can be discovered and rediscovered in the midst of faithful people gathered in God's name to delve into mysteries that are still unfolding.

Delve into Mystery. A need for predictability arises out of human nature. Yet mystery is the very essence of God's nature. Without entering into mystery, we can never know more than we know right now, of God or anything else. Tim Brown cautions that "If you already know what you are after, there is usually not much point in looking" (23). Instead, Ogle reminds us that "creative breakthroughs require leaps into the unknown" (19). In order to make creative breakthroughs, we must be willing to give up the notion that learning takes place on a continuous and linear trajectory, with advances in what we know building incrementally on what we knew before. Instead, making creative leaps can feel more like playing the now-ancient video game Asteroids and pushing the button that made the spaceship disappear and then re-appear at an altogether random other location on the screen. Pushing that button, like leaping into mystery, totally changes the dynamics of the game.[2]

Pay attention to what you pay attention to. Wheatley writes often about the importance of being "disturbed" by the world in the sense of being intrigued or somehow challenged by it. She draws on the work of Humberto Maturana and Francisco Varela who claim that "You can never direct a living system. You can only disturb it" (qtd. in Wheatley, Finding 37). In what ways are you being disturbed? In what ways are you and your church being prompted or prodded to consider change? Richard Ogle suggests that you "Magnify anything that your intuition tells you might be interesting and begin building scenarios around it" (258). Don't settle for being told what's important or for valuing "traditions" just because they have been around a while. In truth, the various ideas presented here will affect each of us differently. Notice what makes you feel charged,

---

[2] National Public Radio's Morning Edition aired a story ("Struggle for Smarts? How Eastern and Western Culture Tackle Learning," November 12, 2012) which examined different attitudes toward intellectual struggle between Eastern and Western cultures. The story looked at ways Eastern cultures value struggle, as evidenced for example by study participants from Eastern cultures being willing to exhaust every resource and their allotted time before giving up on a perplexing problem, while participants from Western cultures tended to give up in thirty seconds on average.

or moves you to the edge of your seat, or sparks a chain of ideas that generate excitement, or inspires a sense of hopefulness. Notice where you feel God in the midst of it all.

Have fun! Church consultant Gil Rendle writes about working with congregations that are "dying of terminal seriousness" (10). Perhaps it is with particular benefit to those congregations that Tim Brown of the innovation firm IDEO writes about the concept of "serious play" (33). In her book, *Perseverance*, Wheatley (151) tells of a busy executive who is talking with her young niece at the end of a particularly hard day. The niece asks, "Did you try hard?" "Yes." "Did you try really, really hard?" "Yes I did." "Well then, now it's time to go out and play." Let playfulness spin you and twirl you and knock you just enough off balance to make life interesting. Let go of the swing and fly through the air. Let laughter help your brain process new information, your body restore health, and your soul find contentment. Don't let yourself forget that delight is a worthy spiritual aspiration, and when all is said and done, joy is a faithful response to God's blessings and God's love.

SUGGESTION: Turn off your GPS and set out on a new and different route home from church next Sunday. Let yourself get lost on purpose. Notice what you notice and enjoy the ride. Pay attention to your new learnings, about the world and about yourself.[3]

Ultimately, what is at stake in opening ourselves to new models of church organization is not only the transformation of the day-to-day functioning of churches as institutions, but also a transformation of the relationship between God and God's churches in the world. Thinking about church organization provides not only opportunities to have more efficient and effective congregations, it also

---

[3] Barbara Brown Taylor has an excellent reflection on getting lost in her book, *An Altar in the World: A Geography of Faith*, HarperCollins Publishers, New York, New York, 2009

creates intersections where people can meet God again for the first time, and even be surprised by God and by each other in the midst of meaningful ministry.

Try this for fun: Write your full name in cursive using the hand other than the one you usually write with. Then continue writing what you're feeling as you do it. What is it like to attempt a familiar task in an unfamiliar way? Can you feel your brain resurging and renewing itself?

_____

_____

_____

7) IMAGINING THE WORLD DIFFERENTLY

Whether we realize it or not, we routinely use the world to make us smarter. For example, we do things like program the phone numbers of family, friends, and colleagues into our cell phone contact lists and look to our car's navigation systems to show us the way to destinations near and far. We also rely on the world to inform how we think and to shape how we live, like when we use ideas from our workplaces to design organizational models for our churches, or when we draw from a set of spoken or unspoken customs to help us know how to behave in church board meetings. Without such guidance, we might, for example, not know how to bring up topics that are important to us in meetings.

By way of such things as technological gadgetry, scientific paradigms, mythical stories, cultural customs, and organizational models, we have systematically endowed the world with more intelligence than it would otherwise have so that it can make us smarter than we might otherwise be.

In his book *Smart World: Breakthrough Creativity and the New Science of Ideas*, Richard Ogle draws from a vibrant body of research to attempt to explain how the world can make us smarter and more creative. His book is a worthwhile stop for anyone on a journey of discovery. It provides an over-arching framework for the reflections that lie ahead, and for the specific activities involved in the whole enterprise of exploring organizational creativity in churches. To benefit from its useful insights, we will do well to understand the basic elements of how the smart world works.

To begin with, Ogle challenges the commonly-held notion that we think inside our heads. It turns out that that is only part of the way things work. He writes that, "The mind – seat and organ of human intelligence – is broader and deeper than we thought; it extends far out into the world, more outside than inside" (13). In making his point, Ogle highlights research that runs counter to what has been labeled the

"MITH myth" – the myth of the Mind-In-The-Head. Instead of being contained within our brains, intelligence and creativity depend on lively interactions with the world beyond our brains – the "extra-cranial world," if you will. Those interactions with the world exponentially expand our potential by dramatically increasing available information and options.

Idea Spaces

The world abounds with what Ogle refers to as "idea spaces." An idea space is "a domain or world viewed from the perspective of the intelligence embedded in it, intelligence that we use – consciously or not – both to solve our everyday problems and to make creative leaps that lead to breakthroughs" (13). More simply, idea spaces are "spaces to think with (15)" that we can tap to expand our own capabilities and understanding.

For example, in his book *Transforming Church Boards*, Charles Olsen suggests multiple ways of incorporating elements of worship services into church board meetings. While Olsen does not talk specifically about connecting idea spaces, *per se*, his suggestions reflect doing just that, taking ideas from one aspect of church life – one idea space, and relating them to another.

The concept of idea spaces might also, as another example, be utilized to help church members seeking to expand their collective notion of congregational leadership. In order to get a broader perspective on the topic, a new idea space might be engaged. The facilitator might infuse the learning process with insights generated by watching and talking about the clip from the animated film Aladdin, where Aladdin invites Jasmine to fly with him on his magic carpet. The scene of the two flying up and down and all around validates the musical claim that, "I can show you the world" and opens up conversation about various aspects of leadership including taking perspective, soothing fear, establishing trust, and experiencing exhilaration.

Even as he claims that thinking extends beyond the brain, Ogle also challenges the notion that genius arises in the brains of isolated individuals solely because they are somehow uniquely endowed with special gifts. There is, Ogle claims, more to it than that. Instead, there are various circumstances that influence what is often perceived as individual accomplishment. To make his point, Ogle (183) tells the story of Gutenberg's printing of the Bible with moveable type, which is widely hailed as an innovative act of genius. In actuality, Gutenberg understood the convergence of circumstances at a particular time, and he seized an opportunity. He picked up where Chinese printing left off – which largely provided the technological foundation for modern printing. He adapted the technology using his exposure to the minting of coins and awareness of already-available techniques and raw materials. And he sought to exploit the ability of his press to provide uniformity of text at a time when the church had mostly settled on which particular texts it would use.

Ogle concludes that "In the end, achieving success in printing was like aligning a Rubik's cube, with now this set of elements, now that coming together in different combinations" (199). Hardly an act of individual genius, then, the mass production of the Bible was the result of Gutenberg's successful linking of ideas spaces which each contained part of the whole but not the whole itself.

We live in a world of ideas that are potential sources of insight and inspiration. Creativity is a matter of navigating the network of idea spaces and integrating disparate learnings into something new and different. Wheatley states that "Innovation is fostered by information gathered from new connections; from insights gained by journeys into other disciplines or places; from active, collegial networks, or fluid, open boundaries" (Leadership 104). Navigating idea spaces is somewhat akin to a painter dabbing a bit of this color and a bit of that to make a new color altogether, or adding a little glitter to make a plain color sparkle.

Particularly creative people are not blinded by conventional wisdom or bound by cultural expectations, but instead free their minds to make new connections. The amount of creativity and innovation is directly related to the degree of separation between idea spaces; the more difference, the greater the effect, and the more innovative the result. But seeing the world differently requires that we summon our courage and liberate our imaginations.

Imagination, Intuition, and Insight

Ogle sheds important light on how creativity works. He highlights the role of imagination, intuition, and insight in making the most of available ideas. Beginning with the assumption that imagination, intuition, and insight are fundamental to creative thinking (3), Ogle explains that imagination helps us to "construct and play with alternative ways of seeing, understanding, and acting in the world that allow something new, interesting, and useful to emerge" (69). Imagination has the power to envision new worlds by freeing us from the "grip of present reality" (69) and reaching "where reason cannot go" (51).

Intuition accompanies imagination and serves as the "navigation system for exploring novel idea spaces" (72). It gives weight to particular ideas that imagination envisions. It is the "gut feeling" that helps differentiate between an idea that is worth exploring and one that is not. Ogle then goes on: "Working together, intuition and imagination give rise to insight, the quintessential phenomenon of breakthrough creativity, the eureka moment, the sudden flash that brings new light to what previously lay in darkness" (72). Imagination, intuition, and insight work together to yield breakthroughs in the creative process.

Analogical thinking underlies that dynamic interaction and provides the mechanism by which ideas spaces are bridged. As opposed to analytical thinking, which relies on reason and works in linear fashion, analogical thinking works by mapping significant structures from a familiar idea space and applying them to a less familiar idea space in ways that make the latter more familiar.

Keith J. Holyoak and Paul Thagard, in their informative study entitled *Mental Leaps: Analogy in Creative Thought*, add that, "The essential requirement for analogical thinking is the ability to look at specific situations and be able to pull out abstract patterns that may also be found in superficially different situations" (19). Those authors break down analogical thinking into the simple but useful labels "source analog" which is the "known domain" and "target analog" which is "a relatively unfamiliar domain" that is yet to be understood (2). We make our way through unfamiliar situations by mapping attributes from what we know to what we don't know, thereby bringing the previously-unknown into clearer focus and closer grasp.

Ogle summarizes that, "Creative leaps arise not from exclusively internal operations of the individual mind (genius or otherwise), but from navigating the idea spaces of the smart world we have built for ourselves; locating the powerful, structured forms of intelligence embedded in them; and analogically transferring these to new spaces" (13). Once that has happened, reason can help make new discoveries more useful. Ogle adds that, "The imagination frees us from the mesmerizing grip of reality, allowing us to invent, play with, and even try out alternative worlds. Only when such an imagined world has come into being can reason go about its work of organizing, structuring, validating, and extending" (73). Reason, then, remains a valuable adjunct to the creative process, though it cannot be creativity's driving force.

Think about a church board that hopes to change the way it conducts its business in order to dispel the air of formality that some members feel diminishes participation and squelches creativity. Rather than drawing from elaborate meeting models used in corporate settings to determine their next steps, or watching C-SPAN for days to capture the finer points of parliamentary procedure, what if the board decided to map from the model of a flowing mountain stream to inform their new way of doing their work? Perhaps their meetings would take on a more crisp and clear and sparkling mood, more dynamic and alive. Maybe ideas would flow more freely and members would, from time to time, even be swept up in the current that brings life to all places it passes.

You might remember the long-famous Reese's Cup advertisements in which one person's chocolate, by some quirk of fate, ended up in another person's peanut butter, and vice versa. The whole episode was messy and each person was annoyed at the other – until they tasted the wonderful flavor of the combination. Perhaps your further reading will feel somewhat like that.

Try this: Take a brief look through the parables of Jesus as told in the gospels. Pay attention to the way those stories use metaphor to help people understand what is less familiar by starting with something they already know well. The parables are an excellent example of analogic thinking in action.

Ogle's description of linking idea spaces offers a useful framework to inform our conversation about organizational dynamics and creativity in churches by providing guidelines for intentionally engaging in creative endeavors. And it is a central idea that supports the inclusion of the next three reflections which draw from three distinct and seemingly disparate idea spaces: living systems, design thinking, and theology.

8) LIVING SYSTEMS

Organizational pioneer Margaret Wheatley asserts that "Every living thing seeks to create a world in which it can thrive" (Finding 66). Life is not about merely surviving, but about thriving on the way toward more abundant life. That is both a promise of our faith, and a vital force behind organizational change. It is a hallmark of an emerging worldview that highlights organizations as living systems.

Paradigms

With an eye toward "creating organizations that are adaptive, creative, and resilient" in the face of pressures from an ever-changing world, Wheatley asserts that, "it is our fundamental way of interpreting the world – our worldview – that must change. Only such a shift can give us the capacity to understand what's going on, and to respond wisely" (Leadership x).

It is now more than a few years since the dawn of the cell phone era. In those early days, I remember young people mysteriously stopping what they were doing to answer calls I didn't even know they were getting. Each time that happened, I had two thoughts: first, they must have really good hearing; and second, I must not. Before I could get to the audiologist, I realized that the cell phone mystery was not about hearing at all. They weren't listening. They were feeling – for vibrations. Having grown up in a world in which phones *rang*, I was unable to appreciate that they could do something else. It turns out that the world had become different than I had always assumed it to be. To adapt, I had to undergo a paradigm shift.

Paradigms are worldviews, ways of thinking about the world or some aspect of it. In Ogle's terms, paradigms are a type of idea space, or space to think with (15). They are overarching conceptual frameworks for making sense of everything that can be made sense of. They include assumptions about how the world works, assumptions so basic that they are easily taken for granted as just the way it is, seemingly ruling out any other ways that it could possibly be.

Paradigms frame the questions we ask and shape the way we ask them. They help to determine what we notice, and they influence what we do in response. They are the light-posts under which we search, as in the familiar story of the man choosing where to look for his keys based not on where he lost them but instead on where the light was. Paradigms are the light by which we see whatever we see, not only in science but in all aspects of life that are quietly but profoundly influenced by prevailing sets of assumptions.

For generations or even centuries, a particular paradigm might be dominant. But in a world that is constantly changing, inevitably, dominant paradigms begin to lose their power to make sense of new discoveries and inform how we live. Paradigms cannot help us cope with information that falls outside of the area upon which they shed light.

Thomas Kuhn, in his classic *The Structure of Scientific Revolutions*, helps us understand the way people reach the limits of a paradigm but keep trying to forge ahead based on what they thought they knew. Caught in a cycle of trying and failing and trying harder, the increased intensity of their attempts to make an inadequate paradigm work generates increased energy. That increased energy can propel the whole system to completely new ways of thinking by means of radical and spontaneous change that results in a new and fundamentally different set of assumptions about the world and how it works. By way of such a process, the old paradigm is left behind and a new paradigm is born. A whole new way of thinking about and living in the world emerges.

For example, a congregation that was known for its extensive involvement in social justice and community service ministries encountered difficulties finding leaders to continue the work. That reality presented a crisis that rippled out into the community; with no group to maintain the program, dedicated money went unspent and needs were unmet. For a number of years, increasingly-frantic efforts were made to re-establish the ministry structure that had been in place, but to no avail. At the same time, however, opportunities for service and requests for funding continued to present themselves. And all of the increased energy resulted in conversations that sparked new ideas. With no formal organizational apparatus to carry on the outreach work in the way it had been done, clusters of individuals banded together to take on particular aspects of the ministry for which they had passion, including ministries focused on feeding, housing, healthcare, and global outreach. Eventually, the ministry was formally reconfigured into a model based on small groups working autonomously rather than one group working all together. Over time, more people became involved in more activities than had ever been the case under the previous model. Late in the process, when a centralized group did come together again, their focus was on communication and facilitation rather than authoritative direction and decision-making. A new paradigm developed spontaneously to replace the old paradigm. In the process, the emphasis shifted from check writing as the congregation's primary means of benevolence to actual hands-on work in the field.

We live now in a time of shifting organizational paradigms. The machine-model paradigm that has prevailed in organizations for centuries is now being challenged by another paradigm that views organizations as living systems. Throughout her work, Wheatley tells what she calls an "ancient new story" (Finding 1) in which we are each summoned to let go of the machine paradigm that has been dominant and instead become yet again "beloved partners with life" (7) by way of a living systems paradigm. We can do so, not by seeking to impose our will on a world that is fundamentally unpredictable and beyond our control, but by discovering and living in harmony with creative forces that are everywhere and always at work in the world. Instead or directing what "should" happen, then, the focus changes to discovering what is already happening and making the most of the opportunities that inherent creativity makes possible.

The emerging paradigm understands organizations as living systems capable of self-creation, purposeful reorganization, and adaptation relative to changing situations and circumstances. The living systems paradigm accommodates the ways the world has changed and is changing since it focuses on sources of understanding that are local and immediate – here and now. Proponents of living systems models remind us that life has indeed been unfolding according to an inherently creative order since the beginning of time. That inherent order is different than imposed control.

While there is no way to approach the comprehensiveness and eloquence of Wheatley's own writings, which I strongly recommend you read if you are at all intrigued or disturbed by what is written here, we can now attempt an introductory overview of key concepts of a living systems worldview. We can lift up those concepts, in particular, that have implications for how churches organize to do their work.

Self-organizing Systems

Front and center in a living systems model is the notion of self-organization which makes it possible for organizations to "stay strong by staying open" so that they might "create structures that fit the moment" (Wheatley Leadership 82). Those structures last only as long as they are useful. Then they go away or are adapted or replaced altogether by new structures that fit the new moment. Self-organization by way of such "process structures" lends itself to organizational agility in a way that fixed, permanent structures in closed organizations cannot.

Wheatley's approach to organizations includes a belief that some might perceive as running counter to all good judgment when she claims that, "organizations that want to stay vital must learn to seek out surprise, looking for what is startling, uncomfortable, and maybe even shocking" (Leadership 108). Those things can knock systems off balance, prompt self-organization as the system's adaptive response, and precipitate new learning; disruptions and disturbances create the context and provide the impetus for growth and change that might not occur in stable systems. The guiding principle underlying the machine model approach, on the other hand, might be best captured in the adage, "If it ain't broke, don't fix it."

Contrary to machine model organizations that strive for equilibrium, open, self-organizing systems make the most of imbalance to bring about adaptation and change. The re-balancing process leads to new learning, perhaps even in the form of finding alternative ways of doing what is to be done. The same can happen in congregations.

Wheatley writes that, "An open organization doesn't look for information that makes it feel good, that verifies its past and validates its present. It is deliberately looking for information that might threaten its stability, knock it off balance, and open it to growth" (Leadership 83). We'll explore later how leadership guru Ronald Heifetz encourages a focus on what he calls "creative deviants," and Tim Brown draws attention to "extreme users" on the edges of the bell curve.

Jeff Patton, in *If It Could Happen Here...*, tells of a small congregation that was "more concerned with survival than with growth" (9). In short, they were more content to look backward with a sense of nostalgia than make significant changes to ensure their longevity. But their desire to stay alive despite dwindling numbers, stagnation and worse prompted a response which included defining a common purpose, connecting with the community, making membership more meaningful, and, gasp!, even getting "beyond committees"(30). Patton remembers that he "continually had to help people out of their comfort zones so they might use their gifts to reach out to others" (30). Reminiscent of Reinhold Niebuhr who drew the distinction between "comforting the afflicted and afflicting the comfortable," Patton adds that he "frequently made people uneasy and uncomfortable." Yet the congregation, and indeed the whole community, responded to the challenge and radically transformed both the church and its circumstances. They became disturbed enough to bring about constructive change.

Identity, Information, and Relationships

Summed up perhaps most succinctly in a chapter entitled "The Irresistible Future of Organizing," written with Myron Rogers and published in *Finding Our Way*, Wheatley identifies three "conditions of self-organizing systems." The first is identity around which systems organize themselves. Identity occupies the central core around which systems revolve. It is to their basic identity that systems refer when confronted with the need to negotiate changes, challenges, and choices. Identity sums up the enduring aspects of the organization that remain when all else is stripped away.

Identity is critical. Wheatley adds that "In organizations, if people are free to make their own decisions, guided by a clear organizational identity for them to reference, the whole system develops greater coherence and strength. The organization is less controlling but more orderly" (Leadership 87). The underlying assumption is that freedom gives people the opportunity to live according to the organizational core identity, without the need for command and control or coercion of any kind. In fact, because they know their own particular circumstances, skills, abilities, and passions, they are able to make better decisions in support of that core identity than if control were imposed from elsewhere in the organization.

The second condition of self-organizing systems, according to Wheatley and Rogers, is information which they refer to as "the nutrient of self-organization" (Finding 39). Information circulates around a system, even giving form to organizations. Information in-forms (Leadership 96). In organizations, information provokes responses that change the system, causing it to adapt and evolve even as it guides that adaptation and evolution. The more information from more perspectives, the richer the view of reality. Accordingly, Wheatley claims that "we need to be constantly asking: 'Who else should be here? Who else should be looking at this?'" (Leadership 66). Who else might have useful information or another perspective to include?

Information, from a living systems point of view, travels in all directions instead of by way of the more traditional unidirectional flow through established channels. Information that bubbles up is at least as valuable as information that trickles down. And information that flows sideways, diagonally, and completely randomly matters too. Indeed Wheatley states often that "people support what they create" (e.g., Leadership 68). In order to fully participate in creating, people need to know what's going on. In healthy, vibrant systems, everybody knows everything all the time.[4]

Networks of <u>relationships</u>, the third condition of self-organizing systems, provide the basis for all interaction such that "*relationship* is the key determiner of everything" (Leadership 10). Relationships are pervasive and essential. Wheatley writes that "None of us exists independent of our relationships with others" (Leadership 35). Drawing on quantum physics, Wheatley reminds us that "different settings and people evoke some qualities from us and leave others dormant. In each of these relationships, we are different, new in some way" (Leadership 35). There are echoes of this same concept in Mary McClintock Fulkerson's notion of a "place to appear" (21), which is "a place to be seen, to be recognized and to recognize the other." It matters where and with whom we find ourselves in relationship and interaction.

In the same way that individuals exist only in relationship, parts exist only in relation to a whole. Unlike machine paradigm thinking that works by breaking things down, living systems thinking works by perceiving things

---

[4] An extreme alternative to information flowing freely and openly around a system, by the way, would be people tightly closing their eyes and mouths and covering their ears. How hard is it for you to imagine that closed approach leading to anything constructive?

together. That shift in thinking fundamentally changes the way we understand the world and our place in it. And it affects the way we think about organizational life as well by requiring that we attend not simply to the various parts of the organization but to how the organization functions as a whole.

Think about the difference between a drawing of a flower on one page and a drawing of the component parts of the same flower arranged in orderly rows on another page. The basic elements of both drawings are exactly the same. While one drawing is easily recognizable as a flower, the other is not. Living systems thinking calls us to observe the parts in relationship with each other in the context of the flower as a recognizable whole. Even when viewing the second drawing, which highlights each part as an individual entity, each is ultimately comprehensible and purposeful only when related to the whole of which it is a part.

In the end, the three conditions of self-organizing systems operate in such a way that, "New relationships connect more and more of the system, creating information that affects the organization's identity. Similarly, as information circulates freely, it creates new business and propels people into new relationships. As the organization responds to new information and new relationships, its identity becomes clearer at the same time as it changes" (Finding 41). By means of the dynamic interaction of identity, information, and relationships, organizations become brand new while staying essentially the same.

Inherent, then, in the interaction of information shared by way of relationships in the context of a core identity is the notion that identity, though stable, is refined through interaction. Interaction is circular, involving multiple sources that constantly feed back into the organization, not linear, building step-by-step. Accordingly, because relationships are nuanced and their intensity is variable, change can happen exponentially rather than proportionately. A classic example of this phenomenon from quantum physics is the claim that a butterfly flapping its wings in Tokyo can cause a tornado in Kansas. Living systems do not operate on the same principle as hitting billiard balls that respond to force and direction in mostly predictable ways. Instead, relationships make it possible for effects to be either bigger or smaller than might be predicted based on calculations of such factors as mass, force, and acceleration. Think of the smile shared in passing that causes a severely depressed person to feel enough of a connection with someone else to reconsider his intention to harm himself.

Borrowing from quantum physics, Wheatley also helps us understand the way our participation in relationships changes those with whom we relate, just as it changes us. There is no "objective reality" *per se*, but only what we observe in a situation which we affect by our very presence. Co-evolution and co-adaptation involve all parties changing and being changed by their interactions.

Wheatley notes that "nothing living lives alone. Everything comes into form because of relationship… Through these chosen relationships, we co-create our world" (Leadership145). You may be aware, for example, that you are a different person when you are with your best friend than you might be with someone you've never met before. This same principle makes it so that a person who in a public gathering rightly says "I'm really very shy" is the life of the party at Thanksgiving dinner. This phenomenon has implications for how we think about interactions within congregations. And it might also inform our theology as well. (More on that in a bit.)

From a living systems perspective, boundaries become meeting places. Wheatley writes that, "complex networks of relationship offer very different possibilities for thinking about self and other. The very idea of boundaries changes profoundly. Rather than being a self-protective wall, boundaries become the place of meeting and exchange" (Finding 48). She continues, "They are the place where new relationships take form, an important place of exchange and growth as an individual chooses to respond to another." There is the familiar colloquialism that also lifts up the paradox of boundaries by claiming that "Fences make good neighbors," not just by limiting access but by creating a point of contact and defining a space for people to be together.

The fundamental dynamic of Wheatley's "new ancient story" is this: "Life is in motion, constantly creating, exploring, discovering. Nothing alive, including us, resists these great creative motions. But all of life resists control. All of life reacts to any process that inhibits its freedom to create itself" (Finding 28). And all of the parents of toddlers and teenagers alike said, "Amen."

C. Kirk Hadaway, in his wonderful book *Behold I Do a New Thing* states that, "the most innovative organizations do not change by anticipating the future. They change by *creating* the future" (6). Thankfully, there are those who have dedicated their lives to fostering creativity and innovation. They are members of an emerging field known as design thinking. And they have practical contributions to make to our conversation about organizational dynamics and creativity in churches.

Hartmut Esslinger, the founder of innovation firm frog, inc., claims that "we are born with the seeds of creativity within us" (xi). Design thinking engages creativity in the service of making the world a better place. It is responsible for much in our world that we easily take for granted, and much that we simply could not live without. In a very real sense, design thinkers stand at the crossroads where imagination, creativity, and reality intersect. They help ideas find embodiment (Brown 35).

Design firms create an environment in which "tender, fresh new ideas" can mature (Esslinger 7). Tim Brown, the CEO of IDEO, writes of design thinking as a "third way" (4) that occupies the space between intuition and rationality. He seems to capture both the practical reality and the spirit of design thinking when he says it is "fundamentally an exploratory process; done right it will invariably make unexpected discoveries along the way, and it would be foolish not to find out where they lead" (16). Design thinkers exude a sense of adventure.

Daniel W. Rasmus, in applying design thinking to workplace experiences, writes that, "Design matters because it creates balance, offers variety and flexibility, and it begs for simplicity and efficiency of movement" (21). Design thinkers develop options for solving problems or meeting needs that may be observed, expressed, or latent, as well as immediate, short-term, or long-term.

Roberto Verganti takes a different approach to design which introduces a new dimension of change. In describing what he calls "design-driven innovation," he asserts that "radical innovation of meaning" is critical to the process. It is not, for him, as much about designing products and services as about shaping the meanings people attach to products and services. Using the introduction of the Wii to the marketplace as an example, he explains how design-driven innovation pushes beyond what people know they want. This is similar to Henry Ford's statement that if he'd have designed what people wanted, he would have designed a faster horse. This approach to design is helpful to keep in mind as we explore innovation relative to church organization. At the very least, it is a reminder that there are possibilities that exist beyond people's immediate field of vision or expressed desires.

Design thinkers are particularly interested in generating ideas. Brown offers this beautiful image of the design thinking process: "Let a hundred flowers bloom, but then let them cross-pollinate" (239). More pragmatically, he notes that while generating ideas, design thinkers engage in "divergent thinking" (66) which works toward naming options and expanding possibilities. Divergent thinking is balanced by "convergent thinking" (66) which seeks to limit options and hone in on choices. The two work together and there are no hard and fast rules about when one way of thinking is appropriate over the other, about when to stop generating new ideas and start narrowing down the ideas that have already been generated. Negotiating the transition from divergence to convergence in the design process relies on many factors including leadership styles, organizational culture, available time and resources, and the degree of patience of participants.

Broad Participation

Similar to the prominence it is given in Wheatley's perspective on living systems, broad participation is a critical aspect of design thinking. Both Wheatley and Brown emphasize participation as a key component of the organizational dynamics that support innovation. Brown begins with the assumption that "all of us are smarter than any of us" (26). He adds that that realization "is the key to unlocking the creative power of any organization." Working all together and intentionally including everyone strengthens organizations.

For Brown, participation extends to the inclusion of clients in the design process. From Brown's perspective, "It's not 'us versus them' or even 'us on behalf of them.' For the design thinker, it has to be 'us *with* them'" (58). That distinction prompts a re-thinking of the relationship between church boards and the congregations they serve, as well as between congregations and the communities they serve.

Underlying this "us with them" approach is a softening of traditional boundaries and an appreciation of the general cultural shift from a consumer economy back to an economy in which people also participate in production. As an example of that consumer-producer shift, Brown describes the transition over time from people listening to music on record albums, to the current situation in which, through available technology and social media, people are once again producing and distributing music themselves. That same cultural shift also influences churches, where the era of pastors, priests, and elected leaders "producing" and other members of congregations "consuming" has largely given way to an age in which members are expected to be as involved in and responsible for the life of the church as designated leaders, especially within Protestantism.

Of course adding more people adds complexity to any process, and that can challenge systems. But the benefits can outweigh the costs. As Brown points out, "Complexity is the most reliable source of creative opportunities" (86). More than adding a few people here or there, Brown suggests paying particular attention, not to people in the middle of the bell curve, but to those on either end where we might expect to find "'extreme users' who live differently, think differently, and consume differently" (44). That can be a significant and very useful change for congregations that are used to dealing with people who are mostly "just like us."

The people on the edges can provide a unique perspective on both what a congregation is at any moment, and what a congregation is becoming. Leadership guru Ronald Heifetz refers to newcomers as "creative deviants" (183) and urges that their voices be heard if organizations are going to be able to see beyond what they currently are. This way of approaching diversity calls into question policies that, for example, require people to have been members of the congregation for a certain amount of time before serving in any official capacity, such as on church boards.

One congregation with such a requirement eagerly awaited the two-year membership anniversary of a man who would have relished being referred to as a "creative deviant." He was immediately elected to the church board once his requisite waiting time was over. Despite having a wealth of ideas to share from a lifetime of active involvement in the church he'd recently left, by the time he was elected, he had become part of the current church culture and had, by then, lost much of the passion behind his new ideas. He had become much less insistent, for example, that a net be put up in the church yard for the youth volleyball league he intended to start. His hopes of reinvigorating the defunct youth program in general had faded, like the hopes of others before him. And, sadly, within months of being elected, he became debilitated by cancer which eventually took his life.

In his memory, the church board did revisit the idea of creating opportunities for new church members to join the board. The conversation included consideration of how much familiarity people should have with current church culture before they can assume a formal position from which they might change it. The group decided that just two of the existing twelve board positions could be opened for new members, while ten positions continued to require longer church membership. The concern was expressed that too many new people could essentially gain enough control to push tradition aside. In such situations, it is sobering to think of what is lost in terms of new ideas and energy that could move churches toward viable futures.

Small, Interconnected Groups

Groups are critical to design thinking, just as networks and relationships are vital from a living systems perspective. Effective teams are interdisciplinary (Brown 27) in that they aim to include diverse perspectives, and they are collaborative, with all responsible for the whole rather than each accountable for a small part of the system that they are charged with representing – or defending as the case may be.

Brown recommends that teams themselves be relatively small but that the various small teams be linked in an interdependent network (29). In such a network, connections are made both within and across groups, information is shared freely and openly, and efforts are coordinated in the service of sparking innovation and fostering further collaboration. In all things, the small groups consider themselves to be part of the whole organization rather than isolated units doing their own work within their own domain.

Prototypes

Once ideas are generated, design thinkers move deliberately to action by developing prototypes or finding other ways to get their ideas into practice. Prototyping is perhaps the most significant practical lesson churches can learn from design thinkers. Brown sums up the value of prototyping by noting that, "The faster we make our ideas tangible, the sooner we will be able to evaluate them, refine them, and zero in on the best solution" (89). Prototypes are not perfect models but are instead "fast, rough, and cheap" (90). Each iteration is part of the process of working toward a better model.

Prototypes are experimental working versions of a desired product. While product designers rely on materials like foam core and glue guns to prototype what they are designing, organizational redesign can involve implementing proposed changes then adjusting once they are in place. Prototyping engages more people with the process sooner and allows for speedier implementation and evaluation of what is ultimately likely to be a better result. It keeps the focus on reality and avoids the creation of elaborate fictions generated by lengthy and untested speculation.

The opening day of Disneyland California is a great example of implementation improving product development. Walt Disney sought to create a theme park different from the dirty and poorly-run amusement parks he visited with his daughters. Yet after years of planning and preparation, opening day of his own creation was a relative disaster. Lines were far too long. Garbage piled up. The intense heat of the day caused the asphalt walkways to soften, resulting in women in high heels sinking into the pavement. Guests were angry and disillusioned. But the actual experience of those problems made it possible to fix them, which Disney surely did and his company has since. In one sense, Disneyland was a prototype upon which Walt Disney World and successive parks around the world have been built, incorporating new learnings with each iteration. Now, Disney parks are among the world's leaders in innovation, customer satisfaction, and brand loyalty.

The Edge of Chaos

Design thinkers and the design process itself remind us that disorderliness accompanies innovation. Brown notes that "insights rarely arrive on schedule, and opportunities must be seized at whatever inconvenient time they present themselves (p. 64)." In general, innovation by way of design thinking processes challenges traditional tendencies toward orderly change. Tom Kelley, also at IDEO, writes that, "We all have a creative side, and it can flourish if you spawn a culture to encourage it, one that embraces risks and wild ideas and tolerates the occasional failure" (13). Yet such talk of risks, wild ideas and failure can undoubtedly rattle peoples' nerves.

Design thinkers talk about living on the "edge of chaos." That is also a common notion that appears throughout contemporary organizational literature and it resonates deeply with Wheatley's work as well. Wheatley writes that "Complex, living systems thrive in a zone of exquisitely sensitive information processing, on a constantly changing edge between stability and chaos that has been dubbed 'the edge of chaos.' In this dynamic region, new information can enter, but the organization retains its identity" (Finding 39). Wheatley and her colleagues who think about living systems, Brown and his colleagues in design thinking, and Rendle writing from within the church together point toward a need to rethink chaos in general.

The word chaos itself can strike fear in the hearts of good and faithful people the world over. But remember that that reaction is residue from a passing paradigm that saw the world as a machine hell-bent on maintaining equilibrium. No doubt chaos is problematic if equilibrium is your goal, but so is any change problematic in that context. New thinking about the world as a living system encourages us to think again about chaos and its relationship with order. Rather than "defeating" order, or winning out over it, chaos instead is a partner with order – and a necessary one at that if systems are to grow and develop.

Wheatley writes that, "It is chaos' great destructive energy that dissolves the past and gives us the gift of a new future. It releases us from the imprisoning patterns of the past by offering its wild ride into newness. Only chaos creates the abyss in which we can recreate ourselves" (Leading 119). Simply put, "the destruction created by chaos is necessary for the creation of anything new."

Rendle states that "Chaos is, in fact necessary" (89). He adds that "The biblical word commonly used to express chaos is *wilderness*, which is the creative place where people are changed."

Chaos is a necessary partner of order in living systems. The "edge of chaos" is a thin space that differentiates one from the other and holds both together. If organizations stray too far into chaos, they risk disintegration. If they settle too much into order, they risk stagnation and death. Rubinstein and Firstenberg help us understand the coexistence of order and chaos by pointing out that, "We have then a choice between two general models: moving from deliberate chaos to emergent order or from deliberate order to emergent chaos" (92). Either way, chaos and order are necessarily linked in the evolution of living systems.

Brown notes that, "Insofar as it is open-ended, open-minded, and iterative, a process fed by design thinking will feel chaotic to those experiencing it for the first time" (17). Yet he offers the reassurance that "over the life of a project, it invariably comes to make sense and achieves results that differ markedly from the linear, milestone-based processes that define traditional business practices."

Perhaps engaging design thinking in organizational redesign is similar to the experience of surfing. Of course staying on the shore seems the safest choice. Riding the waves, on the other hand, involves high levels of risk. But it also offers the possibility of having an exhilarating experience of a lifetime. And if we push that metaphor one step further, we might wonder how safe the shore actually is if water is rising and the beach is eroding; as climate change erodes beaches, so is cultural change eroding the safe places where churches used to be able to safely stand.

If we can re-conceive our relationship with chaos, appreciating it as a necessary partner with order, we might also think again about mistakes and failure, each of which has largely been cast as undesirable from a machine model perspective.

Brown, rather comically, using the metaphor of inviting guests backstage for a theatre performance (i.e., "...Hamlet standing outside the stage door having a cigarette while Ophelia chatters into her cell phone..."), warns that watching design thinking in action can be "messy!" (63). It proceeds in fits and starts and sometimes detours to unexpected destinations. But that is its nature and no reason for fear.

Messiness and mistakes are vital parts of the creative process. They provide evidence of activity and experimentation, and they serve as opportunities for learning. Likewise failure can feed learning and innovation as well. Keith Sawyer, in his book *Group Genius* observes that "many good ideas are needed on the way to that rare great idea" (105). Thomas Edison is famously quoted as having said, "I have not failed. I have discovered 10,000 ways not to make a light bulb."

It is common in the literature dealing with organizational dynamics, creativity, and innovation to find writers celebrating the benefits of making mistakes and risking failure because those experiences have such potential for learning and innovation. Indeed there is much to be said for creating a culture in which people are free to experiment. Experimentation involves feeling safe enough to take risks.

10) JOINING IN CREATION

This book, in one sense, is not about theology at all. In another sense it is entirely about theology and nothing else. I think it might appropriately feel like both. We have and we will continue to venture into territory that is far from where churches have typically travelled relative to thinking about organizational models. But the point of the journey is to find God where one might assume God is, and to seek God where God might otherwise be.

Ultimately, theology is a deeply personal exercise in which we are given the opportunity to come to some notion, valid for this moment alone or enduring through the ages, of God and the great matters of religion. We do so based on what we have been taught, what we have experienced, what is written, what we learn from living faithful lives in the context of church community.

Please consider this preamble an invitation and encouragement to look for God and find God where you will in these pages, in your life, and in your church. I hope you will use what is written here as a series of starting places for your own personal spiritual quest.

As for my own personal starting place, I believe that God is everywhere and always, as much outside sanctuaries as in them, as fully present in church board rooms as in social halls and Sunday School classrooms. God is presumably in mission and justice work, and prayer and song, as much as in moments of congregational conversation and in gatherings for decision-making about things that matter. God is revealed in sacred texts as much as in the changing of seasons and warm hugs and baby smiles. I must confess, however, to not being all that sure that God is made real in bylaws and organizational charts, and policy and procedure manuals. It is incomprehensible to me that God could be confined to diagrams and rigid rules, or that we would try to make it so. Those seem so static and binding while God is dynamic and boundless.

In keeping with the flow of this program in general, it seems worth spending some time reflecting on where we are as we also dare to explore newer ideas.

Biblical God Images

If we page through the Bible, we find that God is always up to something, creating new things out of nothing, turning society up-side-down, providing comfort and causing catastrophe, raising new life out of death. Anthony Robinson writes that, "Scripture tells the story of God's intrusions into our settled worlds, of God's determination to turn over the world as it is and to form a people for God's glory. This God is not in the business of keeping things tidy, nailed down, and predictable. Rather, this is a God who disturbs the status quo, breaks open the settled worlds, reverses the world's order, and raises the dead" (Transforming 23).

When we trace our faith all the way back to its biblical beginnings, we find God at work creating a whole new world out of nothing. Remember the first two verses of Genesis 1: "In the beginning when God created the heavens and the earth, the earth was a formless void and darkness covered the face of the deep, while a wind from God swept over the face of the waters." So from the very first, we are given an image of a creative God, powerful and mighty, and mysterious too.

The idea of something out of nothing seems to be absolutely central to Christian faith and theology as it has been handed down through generations and centuries. The theme lies at the very heart of the story that lies at the very heart of who we are as Christians. In the same way that God is capable of creating something out of nothing, we learn that God is also capable of raising new life after death. Resurrection comes only after death just as Easter Sunday comes only after Good Friday.

Yet when it comes to church organization under the old machine model, formless voids are generally not desirable and institutional death is typically something people try to stay away from. I wonder if we miss something when we side-step or ignore those miraculous something-out-of-nothing, life-after-death stories of our faith that lend credence to living systems perspectives. Those stories offer hope when all seems lost – which seems a timely message for churches worried about what comes next and wondering whether to keep doing what they're doing or try something else altogether. What do those stories tell us about holding on, and about letting go?

Many stories of journey fill the Bible's pages, from Abraham and Sarah venturing to a far-off land, settling in, then departing again for yet a new home. The Exodus story describes at some length a wilderness journey and tells of a small group of pilgrims overcoming much travail to reach the Promised Land. Gil Rendle, who draws on that story as a guiding metaphor for his excellent book, equates that journey with a time of chaos and uses the metaphor to help explain the times in which we now find ourselves. We know that biblical journeys usually involved venturing off into unknown places – which people did, if sometimes hesitantly or even grudgingly. Does your congregation have that same spirit that compels you to set aside what you have known in order to try new things, walk new paths, and forge new futures? Are congregations generally up for the sheer hassle of it all? Do they have a choice?

Along the way, we discover God as a refuge, a fortress, a comforter even in times of desperation. Angels seem to always be close at hand, waiting to proclaim those powerfully reassuring words "Be not afraid" that help person after person negotiate challenging situations, make hard choices, and find new direction.

Self-surrender is posed in contradiction to a world in which people are generally trying to claim personal power and authority. Throughout the stories of Jesus' life, faithful discipleship is defined paradoxically as giving away rather than storing up treasures, giving up life to save it. Pride of place is challenged as the preferred way to relate to others. Jockeying for status proves futile. Is your congregation organized around getting or giving away? How is status measured?

We are reminded that God is in charge and that God commanded us to "Be still, and know that I am God." The notion of getting out of God's way takes hold in religious teachings if not always in people's daily lives. It seems a critical consideration in church organization is whether we really make room for God to be God. Or is congregational organization the domain of church life in which we are content or compelled or required to assert more of ourselves? How much of God's creative movement are we really willing to tolerate? Would we know that movement if we saw it with our own eyes?

Jesus brings a new covenant and sets out to change the world. His teachings challenge the way things are, putting the first last and the last first, reaching out to people on the margins of society, demonstrating a whole new way to be faithful. What courage we witness in those who broke with what had always been to give birth to a brand new idea that is now our ancient faith.

As we follow the biblical story further, the early church comes into existence and eventually overcomes fear to point toward a new way forward. The first Christians do their best to maintain a sense of purpose carried on from their days with Jesus in the Galilean countryside.

The teachings of our faith help us to know that God is capable of making all things new. Do our congregations live like that is true? Who's really in charge? God? The church board? Church members? Which ones? Can new things really happen anyway?

Wheatley puts in words what others of us might also believe: "I want to trust in the universe so much that I give up playing God. I want to stop struggling to hold things together. I want to experience such serenity that the concept of 'allowing' – trusting that the appropriate forms will emerge – ceases to be scary. I want to surrender my fear of the universe and join with everyone I know in an organization that opens willingly to its environment, participating gracefully in the unfolding dance of order" (Leadership 25). That kind of hope would seem to have grand implications for what it means to live a life of faith, and what it means to organize churches.

Bundles of Potentiality

Wheatley describes people as "bundles of potentiality" (Leadership 35), made real in moments of interaction with others. I wonder if God is that way too, more real in interaction with us than at other times. To be sure, God is more real *for us* in our interactions with God. I'm not at all saying that God doesn't exist outside of our interactions, but where is God when we are not mindful of God?

I think the prospect of bringing God to life by way of interactions can inform and enliven church organization. We know that God is "where two or three are gathered." *That* we have already been promised. Church organization is a way of making sense of gatherings of two and three and sometimes many more. How would it change church organization if we conceived of it as discovering, designing and bringing to life a network of relationships that bring us closer to God, that make God more real, that bring our churches into closer contact with God and God's call upon our life together?

Think about this. Quantum physics, from which Wheatley draws some of her ideas, asserts that the way we interact with the world changes the world. In that sense, there is no such thing as an "objective" view of a world "out there." The mere observation changes the observed and the observer alike; the two co-evolve into something that is uniquely the product of the interaction. It matters what we notice. And being noticed matters. It could even be said that the interaction is life-giving in that it gives birth to an instance of life that otherwise would not have occurred.

Wheatley writes that, "None of us exists independent of relationships with others. Different settings and people evoke some qualities from us and leave others dormant. In each of these relationships, we are different, new in some way" (Leadership 35). Is it possible that church organization has the potential to make God more real? Does God become incarnate, embodied somehow, in and by way of the networks of relationships that exist within and beyond congregations? Would it change anything if we knew that were true?

Church Organization as a Theological Act

Why such theological ruminations matter here in this program about re-thinking church organization is that, in important ways, what we are doing is indeed about God, and discovering God in the midst of our ministry settings. It's easy sometimes to think about church organization as the necessary "business" side of church life, something to do because it has to be done – before getting back to the really important stuff. But what if... What if we were to think about church organization as a deeply theological act that has the potential to open up – or to close off – fresh, new encounters with God?

Let's revisit the fundamental assumption I put forward at the opening: The way congregations organize themselves to do their work is as much a theological act as anything else they do, and it has impact on everything else they do. Do you believe in a God for whom that might be the case?

There is a dual challenge to church organization if we accept that it is a theological act. The first challenge has to do with making room for God as a living, moving, creative presence capable of more than we can comprehend or control, beyond what we can contain in rules and structures. Specifically with regard to the organizational life of churches, is God allowed to be God on God's terms or is God limited by other constraints that people create and impose? The second, and quite-related challenge has to do with getting ourselves out of the way enough for God's presence to make a difference. In the balance is a decision about whether God is going to be God or we are in matters of church organization. God being God requires that we avoid imposing our own desires and agendas on what's happening, and that we develop patience and attentiveness to what God is already doing all around us, and to what God might be doing next.

If we dedicate ourselves to discovering God and making space and time for God in the organizational life of churches, church organization is no longer a distraction from "what really matters," but a worthy spiritual quest in its own right. In any case, it seems fair to say that God is worthy of more attention than is possible in what Charles Olsen refers to as "book-end" prayers to begin and end church board meetings (Olsen Transforming 20).

Ponder this: Wheatley writes that "By observing with new eyes the processes of creation in us, we can understand the forces that create galaxies, move continents, and give birth to stars" (Finding 24).

What might it mean for you to imagine yourself as a co-creator with God? Do you dare assume that it could be so? If it is, how might that change your thinking about God and about yourself?

SECTION THREE: DISCOVERING NEW WAYS

So what does it all mean? How might we be different as a result of reflecting on these ideas?   What might we actually do differently?   The next five reflections are intended to provide a useful framework for moving ahead with ways your congregation might more nimbly organize to do the work to which you are called. The first reflection deals with identity expressed as common purpose as a key center around which all else revolves. The next sections explore ways to organize and operate in a manner that frees you to do the work that awaits you. In the closing reflections of this section, leadership is redefined and tinkering is extolled as a way of life.

11) COMING TOGETHER PURPOSEFULLY

Maybe you have heard the story about the man who, on his way to work one morning, encountered another man asking for food. The first man took the second man to his church, thinking surely the pastor would be able to help. But the church office was closed. So the first man took the second man to a local restaurant for breakfast, and made sure he had a little food for later. And they went on their separate ways. The first man wondered, though, where the pastor was.

The two men encountered each other again the next day. This time, the second man was asking for a coat for winter. So they again walked to the church office, which was again closed. A bit irked at the pastor but still intent on helping, the first man walked the second man to the neighborhood thrift shop and bought him a coat, and a hat and scarf too.

On the third day, the two men met yet again. Now the second man was in need of housing. Again they walked the now-familiar path to the church office which, unbelievably, was closed this time too. The first man swore that he'd let the pastor have it when he saw him on Sunday. Then he walked the man to the local cold weather shelter where they would help him find housing for the night and a more permanent place to live.

Well, Sunday came, and the first man entered the church and stormed right to the pastor's office. He told the pastor all that had happened and angrily asked the pastor why he hadn't been around. He said, "I was sure the church could help that man!" The pastor replied, "It sounds like the church did help him."

The man was part of a congregation that had long given priority to serving the local community through mission and outreach. The congregation was part of a denomination that had pioneered programs to help poor people all around the world. On every level, there was a shared common purpose that the man referenced and lived out. When confronted with the situation of a person in need, the man did not have to ask what he should do, but only to figure out the best way to do it given the situation.

Common Purpose

In introducing the title concept in his book *Common Purpose*, Joel Kurtzman writes that "Common purpose is what turns *me* into *we*... It is a feeling that we're all in this together and that we all know and understand what to do, why we're here, and what we stand for" (xxi). He adds that "common purpose is not just a feeling; it's a force" (xxiii). Indeed common purpose can serve as a central organizing force in congregations by setting a guideline to which people can refer as they do the work of the congregation's ministry in the circumstances in which they find themselves.

Living systems revolve and develop around a common purpose that guides situational decision-making and makes it possible for organizations to move toward life that is both richer and more abundant. Common purpose makes it so that organizations don't need to "sweat the small stuff" but can instead let all things work for good in terms of what really matters. Congregations that know what they have set out to do together don't have to regulate behavior or generate prescriptive procedures. Because they know what the common purpose is, people are free to work toward it in ways that make sense given the realities they encounter, creating possibilities and bringing to bear resources that might never have been anticipated in writing any kind of "how to" manual on ministry or church life.

Wheatley writes that, "Clarity of purpose at the core of community changes the entire nature of relationships within that community. These communities do not ask people to forfeit their freedom as a condition of belonging. They avoid the magnetic pull of proscribing behaviors and beliefs, they avoid becoming doctrinaire or dictatorial, they stay focused on what they're trying to create together, and diversity flourishes among them" (Finding 50). And it is that diversity that makes novel solutions possible; it is a potential source of tremendous vitality. Rather than limiting people's choices, being clear about common purpose sets the backdrop against which people can discover new ways of being and, thus, become more fully alive and more fully engaged.

By means of what Wheatley terms "self-referencing," every self-organizing system refers back to its core identity and common purpose in response to challenges and choices so that "it always changes in such a way that it remains consistent with itself" (Leadership 85). Accordingly, Wheatley adds that, "Change is never random; the system will not take off in some bizarre new directions. Paradoxically, it is the system's need to maintain itself that may lead it to become something new and different" (85). But a lively and living sense of core identity and common purpose remain at the center of the changed organization.

Who we think we are shapes who we will become and what we will do as congregations. In that sense, common purpose functions like a paradigm or worldview that influences what we notice, how we understand what we notice, and what we do with our new learnings. Common purpose is an idea space from which we can draw useful information about what to do when we are not sure.

There is an old axiom that says, "You've got to stand for something or you'll fall for anything." Congregations have got to stand for something, and that something is what is central to the congregation's sense of itself. Common purpose becomes then the reference point for making all decisions, like those having to do with developing programs, allocating funds, employing and deploying human resources, and taking any action on all levels of church life.

Establishing a common purpose is not the same as writing a mission statement or a vision in the way those are often done. A common purpose does not hinge on listing specific activities to do together over the next several years or mapping out goals for future achievement. Those can and will inevitably change according to circumstances that cannot be foreseen at the outset. More central to defining common purpose are the following questions that Wheatley informs: First, what do we know about ourselves as a congregation right now? Part of developing that self-understanding can involve exploring related questions about what is life-giving as opposed to life-draining, what is good about this congregation as it exists today, and what resources are naturally available and ready to use. Second, what can we do now that we're together? Discerning what to do together can include expanding awareness of opportunities that are presenting themselves and being sure to notice where life is happening already in ways that provide both a foundation and momentum for further action.

Even when congregations commit to producing a mission statement or writing a vision, it is tempting to just plow through the process until the job is done, or in time to meet a deadline or at least somebody's expectations. It is not uncommon for that work to be done primarily by a set-apart committee charged with leading the way. In living systems, however, it is vitally important that whole congregations agree – thoughtfully, prayerfully, mutually, genuinely – upon a common purpose that reflects their core identity and reason for being together. Rubinstein and Firstenberg, in their book *The Minding Organization*, state that "Purpose pulls all of the trajectories of motion in the complex organization into a shared orbit" (19). It is around a common purpose that all other activities of congregations cohere.

Getting to common purpose is about much more than undertaking even an exhaustive self-assessment, grasping the demographics of a community, polling the congregation, or surveying the latest trends in church growth and vitality. While those activities might generate data and provide concrete numbers to which congregations might cling, they might well miss the mark in terms of recognizing what is already authentically life-giving in congregations. Those methods use blunt tools that are readily misapplied to situations in which nuanced understanding is of greater benefit. They objectify what is inherently subjective and externalize what is inherently internal. And they can be used to side-step the important process of people actually talking with one another about what matters most in their life together.

Getting to common purpose is about listening to the future from a place that is truly grounded in the present. While that takes time, it is both possible and critically important. An upcoming "resource reflection" ("Presencing") outlines work done by Peter Senge and his colleagues who have developed a process for doing just that kind of listening to the future from the present. It begins with a sense of wonder, pushes for deep understanding, and moves to deliberate action. Naming a common purpose also necessarily involves hearing and accounting for each and every voice. It requires that all participants set aside assumptions, presuppositions and agendas to work toward something new that can only emerge collectively. (Another upcoming resource reflection explores Conversation and its role in congregational life.)

Making the Most of Messiness

Life in any organization can get complicated and messy from time to time. We know that conflict emerges even (especially?) in organizational systems in which order is imposed and control is assumed. The same is true in organizations that specifically encourage autonomy around a common purpose. There are likely to be points of tension that, on one hand threaten the organization, yet on the other hand provide opportunities to strengthen the community and further clarify the common purpose.

Consider this story of how common purpose can play out in congregations. Three individuals who had agreed to be involved in adult Sunday School programming created and offered to facilitate a year-long course especially for adult "seekers" who may have disengaged from church in general or who may have never been engaged with church in the first place. The intent was to create an open conversational forum for people to address questions in dialogue with each other and with the denomination's stance on important issues. Because of the program's focus, it was assumed that current members would also benefit from participation.

In order to reach the primary intended audience, an ad campaign was developed using a series of new logos designed to transform outsider's views of the congregation that might only have been based on the utterly traditional church building that is the congregation's most visible physical presence in the community. An artist was commissioned to come up with the logos. Against the backdrop of a colorfully reproduced silhouette of the church building, one of the designs had balloons attached to the steeple as if they were lifting the building off the ground. Another colored the church with a bright rainbow. A third showed a bold star-burst across the front of the building. Each design had a whimsical charm.

The team loved the drawings, though each member had her or his favorite. However, as the ads ran in the newspaper, it became clear that, while many people appreciated the campaign and the program it announced, some others truly did not like the images as public representations of the congregation. There was rampant parking lot conversation about how the ads got into the newspaper in the first place. "They make us look kooky! Who approved those?!" It turns out that no one had actually "approved" them outside of the team that prepared them. There was a moment of tension that created a need for the community to delve further into its self-understanding.

Two aspects of the ad campaign were talked about at the next church board meeting. The first was communication. Even though the board generally appreciated the ads and their intent, they would have appreciated knowing they were going out. Information is, after all, a nutrient to living systems as Wheatley points out. Pre-emptive communication that enlisted the council's and the congregation's ideas and provided an opportunity for conversation would have likely headed off what eventually presented as conflict.

The second question relates to whether the ads were appropriate for the congregation. When the ads were viewed in light of the congregation's common purpose, people realized that the ads were entirely in line with the congregation's expressed purpose to "be a church for all people" that "invites people into Christian covenant." "All people" presumably includes those seekers for whom the ad campaign was created.

There are undoubtedly multiple ways to make sense of the situation with the ads. One way is to simply think through how the existence of an expressed common purpose freed people to act, within the field of vision of their particular part of the congregation's overall ministry. The team was empowered and inspired, and their efforts yielded positive results – both with people who were already members, and with some who actively explored membership soon after they began participating in the program. Now, among its standard public representations which tend to highlight the beautiful steeple, the congregation has access to new options that emerged out of a different stream of creative thought but support the common purpose nonetheless.

In the midst of disagreement about the ads, the situation prompted healthy conversation that included people who might not have been as fully engaged were it not for their discontent. The controversy provided an opportunity to have a fuller conversation about the church and its common purpose, to share divergent points of view, and to arrive again at a refined shared commitment.

Looking Higher

Be sure to look beyond your congregation in setting your common purpose, to have in mind some sense of the very highest purpose for which you are together. Recall Jesus' focus on changing the world and caring for poor and needy people, loving those on the margins of society, bringing God's kingdom to everyone. It really is all well and good for churches to be made up of "nice people" who care for each other, or for your congregation to be something like a "warm and welcoming family." Each of our journeys is surely made easier when we are part of a community that loves us and cares for us. However, churches ultimately do not exist only to take care of their own, though that is an easy habit to fall into. Somewhere along the way, it became harder for good church people to say to one another "It's not about you." That may be because it's also hard to acknowledge that "It's not about me either." Defining common purpose lies somewhere beyond all of that and the grand obsessions that can needlessly throw discipleship off track. Perhaps you can pick the petty thing that your congregation has been tempted to ball itself up about lately. Was it worship style, music selection, the altar flowers, the pastor's new hair-do, or what? You are better than that. Get past it. There is so much that matters so much more. Look higher.

HOW TO GET TO COMMON PURPOSE: Aim for a simple, concise, one-line statement. Taken together, the final two reflections in this compilation (labeled "Resource Reflections") can set the stage for defining your congregation's common purpose and engaging the process by way of conversation. You might consult those reflections at this point and think through how to use them to bring as many people as possible together to name and claim who you are and what you are going to do together right now. Once you have arrived at a statement, proclaim it boldly and broadly so that everyone can say it, know it, and live it.

While I am hesitant to provide any sort of template for a statement of common purpose – there are unlimited possibilities, I offer that your common purpose might begin with "We are..." followed by some central descriptor of your congregation. That can then be followed by a second phrase that starts with "that..." and expresses what you have set out to do in response to God's call upon your church for now. For example: "We are an Open and Affirming congregation that makes a difference."

Then, by all means, keep paying attention to what you have come up with. Stay alert to the need for ongoing conversation to refine what you have agreed upon. Think in terms of iterations. Remember that the prototype you come up with for your common purpose will continue to evolve, so be willing to engage the process again and again to keep it relevant. At least once per year, for example, make sure you intentionally come back to the process and that you are still all on the same page, or decide together that the page has turned. Is your purpose still common, and is it still relevant?

Somewhere at this very moment, someone is thinking about how their church is organized. Even if not in such terms, they are thinking about the way boxes relate to one another, who is accountable to whom, and who is responsible for what. This box reports to that box. These people need to know this but not that, and they surely shouldn't know about the other thing. It is an exercise in perseverance to determine how things should fit together. Sadly, it is ultimately also likely to be an exercise in futility. From the moment the ink hits the paper to draw a box in the chart, the person who would be confined to that box pushes out and bursts free to do something that may well be as necessary as it is unexpected. One person might say something like, "If only people would stay in their boxes!" (Or, "If only they would do what they're supposed to do!") Another person might ask, "Why do they have to be in boxes in the first place?! Let's see what good they're up to instead."

Process Structures

Consider this: "How do you hold a hundred tons of water in the air with no visible means of support? You build a cloud" (Cole qtd. in Wheatley Leadership 90).

Different situations require different responses. Yet churches have often organized into structures that last generations and that may or may not be designed to respond adequately to emerging developments and needs. Brown asserts that "Instead of an inflexible, hierarchical process that is designed once and executed many times, we must imagine how we might create highly flexible, constantly evolving systems in which each exchange between participants is an opportunity for empathy, insight, innovation, and implementation" (187). Brown's thoughts point to what Wheatley refers to as "process structures." Process structures are flexible responses to the demands of particular situations, circumstances, and opportunities. They emerge locally to meet particular challenges and choices, then give way to new, emergent structures to meet the next set of circumstances that arise.

Wheatley writes about process structures this way: "The viability and resiliency of a self-organizing system comes from its great capacity to adapt as needed, to create structures that fit the moment. Neither form nor function dictates how the system is organized. Instead, they are *process structures*, reorganizing into different forms in order to maintain their identity. The system may maintain itself in its present form or evolve to a new order, depending on what is required. It is not locked into any one structure; it is capable of organizing into whatever form it determines best suits the present situation" (Leadership 82). In a sense, process structures are like water in a stream that flows freely, bending, zigging left and zagging right, moving back and forth on its way toward its destination. Quite obviously, water flows in a fluid manner. Nimble churches organize themselves with that same fluidity, flexibility and openness to do what it takes to get where they are going.

Following receipt of a significant bequest, the local congregation that set out to make a difference resolved to explore three specific aspects of church life that related to their common purpose. Three groups were formed – you can call them "task forces, "work groups," "play groups," "ministry teams," or whatever label works for you. Each group focused on a particular new program or emphasis. Despite perennial problems with getting enough people to serve on ongoing boards and committees, fully forty people stepped up to serve energetically on the focused task forces. And each task force developed its own organizational model using process structure concepts as a general guideline. From the outset, each group was given a task and then set free to accomplish it. They were given ongoing support by the church council and the congregation, but they were not burdened with explicit directions.

The group responsible for helping the congregation explore issues related to becoming Open and Affirming met as needed for approximately one year. They worked at times as a whole group and at other times in smaller groups or pairings to provide relevant learning opportunities and programs related to the topic. And they brought the congregation to a vote – which overwhelmingly favored Open and Affirming. Then the group disbanded. In their place, a brand new group emerged spontaneously, more than a year later, to radically live into the vote, this group a broad constellation of individuals from the church and wider community who discovered each other after years of doing parallel work. This new group came together following one simple phone call made by one person concerned about bullying, and rather instantly became a powerful and growing network of connections that countless earlier efforts failed to evoke.

A second group was charged with establishing a foundation to give regional, national, and global grants to address systemic issues related to social justice. The initial group developed the process by which applications would be solicited, decisions would be made, and funds would be disbursed. Then they reconfigured the group for the issuance of the first grants, with some members staying on, some going off, and new members joining. That group is now preparing for its fifth configuration and is planning to address newly emerging questions about how their work can be more thoroughly integrated into the life of the congregation.

A third group was put in charge of a significant building project that eventually took shape as a construction and renovation project aimed at creating a space that could be used by the wider community. That group vigorously sought information from all involved building users and from the congregation, distilled that information, engaged a design-builder, and presented a plan which was approved and acted upon by the congregation. While maintaining a unified organizational core, members also worked in sub-groups and individually for parts of the project, and their affiliations were driven by their interests, skills and passions. At the moment actual work began, the group shifted day-today management of the project to an identified member who coordinated with the design-builder through the remainder of the project. It turns out that the opportunity for daily project management became available right as an experienced government contractor retired and was looking for something to do with his time. The various specialized sub-groups remained active to support the project, and the whole group remained in place to respond as needed with various decisions. Then they, too, disbanded when the building was complete and occupancy permits were secured.

Each group adapted freely to meet the charge they were initially given. Those initial charges, which were derived from the congregation's common purpose, identified what each group was to do but not how they were to do it. And all of the groups were outrageously successful. Each became a "place for the exchange of energy" (Wheatley Leadership 72), able to do its work free of overly-intrusive hierarchy or highly-prescribed directives. Keith Sawyer writes in support of such an approach: "The most innovative teams are those that can restructure themselves in response to unexpected shifts in the environment" (17). And the self-driven evolution of each team fostered a profound sense of responsibility within the groups that was in concert with the overall ministry of the congregation. (It is worth noting that the autonomous functioning of the three task groups also allowed the church board to support multiple major projects simultaneously without undue stress and strain.)

Utilizing process structures may be the single biggest factor that increases flexibility and helps congregations become organizationally nimble. But they typically cannot be mapped out in advance and, by definition, they cannot be set in place in perpetuity. They also cannot simply be mere adaptations of what is already in place. They emerge in real situations and are responsive to changes in the environment. Ogle (21) writes about the way paths emerge on new campuses. Rather than building paths in from the start, designers often let them emerge as a result of how people naturally make their way from place to place. Designers then build more stable walkways where informal ones have already shown them to be useful. If patterns of usage shift, new walkways are built to accommodate them so that the landscape becomes something completely different. Church organization can be done the very same way.

Bruce Sanguin in his book *The Emerging Church* writes of "Ministry anywhere, anytime, by anybody" (174). He continues, "An organizational model needs to signal that we're all 'ministers' and therefore all responsible for taking ministry initiative. If God is calling an individual or team to do something, let's make the turn-around-time as fast as possible." He lifts up the value of clearing away bureaucratic clutter for the sake of facilitating lived ministry.

One way to think about the difference between process structures and fixed structures is to think about the difference between Velcro and glue. Like Velcro, process structures create the possibility of connecting, disconnecting, and re-connecting with relative ease. Fixed structures like organizational charts and standing committees rely on glue to hold them together; it's usually possible to get them apart if you have to, but it's not easy to do without extensive collateral damage. If you have to draw an organizational diagram, use pencil rather than pen so adaptations can easily be added when they occur.

Connecting the System to Itself

Process structures are connected by way of the multi-level network of relationships within which and out of which they emerge. Remember that relationships between the various entities in a system are the basic building blocks of life according to Wheatley and Rogers. No group or individual within a congregation exists in isolation. Each is part of a larger whole and each is connected to all of the other parts. Sometimes those connections are easily traceable. Sometimes they are less obvious. But they are always there.

As a general principle, Wheatley suggests that it is worthwhile to connect systems with themselves (e.g.,

Leadership 145). Creating opportunities for dynamic interaction increases the complexity of the organization, and thereby makes the organization stronger, more durable, and more sustainable. For example, one church developed a meeting format in which all of the named groups and identified ministries in the church met together on the same night each month, beginning with a communal supper, continuing through each group's meeting, and ending with a gathering of the group leaders to share information and ensure coordination of activities and events. While the format created some difficulties for people who were committed to multiple groups, the collective gathering times made it possible for people to build and strengthen relationships, feel connected to the larger whole, and even generate excitement together. Having various meetings going on simultaneously in the same area also improved communication and collaboration across teams and throughout the congregation.

Communication is always central to the healthy functioning of organizations, and its role probably cannot be over-estimated. Think about recent national and world events that bring the importance of communication to our collective attention. The Occupy Movement, for example, was largely facilitated by effective communication that allowed for networking and the forming of new connections. The uprising now known as the "Arab Spring" also heavily relied on communication to lend a sense of solidarity to revolution. Approached from the other direction, it is often the case that governments that want to squelch protests first limit communication or make it impossible for people to communicate with each other. Communication matters.

In the same way that it is useful for families to share meals together, it is useful for groups and individuals to have opportunities to reaffirm connections with organizations as a whole – particularly when food is involved, but even when it's not. Networks of relationships are life-giving and life-affirming. They help people locate themselves in the world and connect with something larger than themselves; what better antidote for people seeking a sense of belonging. There was a time when my youngest daughter used to run down the hallway ahead of me when I picked her up from school each afternoon. Invariably she would end up waiting for me outside the main office where she gazed at the school mascot mural which was made up of hundreds of tiny little photographs of each of the students in the school. She would locate her picture and she appreciated being able to see herself as one of many, as part of a whole. Do we need a reminder that being connected with others in meaningful ways is an inherent and very basic human need?

The world can be visualized as a vast web of connections. Take time to notice that every single interaction in an organization takes place at the precise point where two or more entities converge within the network at a given time. Though they can easily be taken for granted, those intersections become places of meaning and even magic. Yet the web extends far beyond particular interactions.

Just as relationships exist within the congregation, so do they also extend outward in the form of wider church connections with clusters of local churches, for example, and with formal denominational bodies. From there, connections extend by way of the Universal Church to the world, and into the solar system and out into the universe and beyond. In the same way that a rising tide raises all boats, strengthening those connections strengthens the whole network and all whose existence depends upon it.

Sawyer (185) tells the story of two different approaches to innovation that can help churches rethink the ways they engage broader networks. The story compares the experiences of Boston on the east coast and what is now known as the Silicon Valley on the west coast. Both places had the potential to be the hub of the home computer industry back in its earliest days. But whereas the computer companies ringing around Boston took a very proprietary approach to sharing ideas, creating structures and rules to ensure that information remained within each company, the folks in Silicon Valley openly shared information by way of casual contacts between workers and through more formal consultations about new possibilities and nagging problems. The result was that the companies in Silicon Valley were able to make more progress faster, and to connect to emerging markets more effectively because they were already connected to each other. In the end, Silicon Valley won out, and the Boston computer industry finished a distant second.

Churches that intentionally and thoughtfully connect with each other can become stronger in general. They exponentially expand their available resources and can even make the impossible possible through the exchange of information, ideas, and shared commitment. Making connections helps to ensure the well-being of congregations individually and collectively, and it works toward the vitality of the church on all of its levels.

Wheatley writes that "in this exquisitely connected world, it's never a question of 'critical mass.' It's always about *critical connections*" (Leadership 45*)*. Networks magnify and amplify the impact of events in such a way that very small events can have enormous impact.

Among all else that they do, networks can spark and cultivate creativity. Our connections with others make our lives what they are, in big ways and small. And you never know what will make a difference. As I was preparing the initial table of contents for this collection of reflections, I was struggling with how best to organize the information I hoped to share. Sitting off in a corner of the room, sighing now and then, I guess I seemed sufficiently troubled that my oldest daughter asked what I was puzzling over. Once I told her, she quietly went back to her own work and I to my consternation. Within minutes, she returned with a drawing of a literal table with packages stacked on top of it. She gave me another way to think about a "table of contents." Her sharing of her idea was just the new connection I needed to unlock my creative energy so that my ideas could flow more smoothly. If I had remained on my single, solitary path, I am quite sure my brain would have tired before resolving the impasse.

Practical Suggestions for Organizing Nimbly:

1) Relax membership requirements so that your congregation can draw upon the gifts, talents, and energy of people who are willing to commit to active participation on different terms. Is maintaining formal membership protocols more important than engaging gifted people in vital ministry?

2) Make it possible for people to use their gifts without having to progress through arbitrary steps to eventually end up in the right place. If, for example, someone is good with money, let them deal with money. If someone is a gifted spiritual leader, let them be just that without having to "do time" doing something else first. Abandon hierarchies that arbitrarily create unnecessary steps for people to negotiate before they can serve in the ways they are called.

3) Reconsider "terms" for leadership and volunteer positions. Create opportunities for people to give what they can, for as long as they are willing and able. Then give them free and open permission to step back when they need to and opportunities to come back when they can. Think more about getting things done with the best people you can find at a given moment rather than filling slots because they are there.

4) Create opportunities for many groups to be together in the same space as they do their work. Doing so opens up the possibility of dynamic interaction between different parts of the congregation and lends itself to an over-arching sense of shared identity and common purpose.

5) Get church board meetings out of the board room and into wide open spaces where anyone who wants to participate can fit and have a seat at the table. Extend invitations for anyone to come and join in. You are all in this together, so act like it. Or meet in some place different all together – like in the church

yard, or on a mountain top, or beside a flowing stream. Imagine the ways the tone and direction of conversations might change in light of the new context.

Use this open space to list other ideas for organizing nimbly:

13) OPERATING DYNAMICALLY

Richard Ogle observes that, "Belief in the necessity of centralized control dies hard... We still find it very hard to tolerate situations where things are seemingly out of control or don't really make sense, and where unanticipated outcomes are the norm. But this is exactly what an emergent situation is; that is, one where the major elements and the principles governing their alignment are not being formulated from a centralized authority, but are an outcome of the *self organizing dynamic of the space as a whole*" (112). Rather than being locked into pre-established patterns, emergent, self-organizing congregations thrive because they are constantly seeking and always responsive to new information from the whole organization in the context of the wider world.

As you make your way into the next few pages, remember the simple truth that no two churches are the same; each is uniquely blessed and called to its very own unique mission and ministry in its own place and time. As you organize to operate dynamically, know that no church can do everything but every church can do something.

Covenant Guides

Operationally, the primary task for churches is to organize in support of what they say they do, to make sure they are set up to work toward their common purpose. Doing so requires thinking through the ways the common purpose can best be lived out in real life by real people. Instead of over-regulating and becoming prescriptive, you might consider creating a "Covenant Guide" that concisely describes how your congregation agrees in global terms to live its life together in light of what you have agreed is most important.

People in the various small groups will benefit from knowing the larger purpose of their work but they do not need to be directed in the particular ways they must carry it out. Rather than enumerating specific and detailed requirements for every function that can be anticipated – which, of course, inevitably falls far short of describing everything that will actually need to be done, covenant guides translate the common purpose in terms of critical areas of church life, and they prepare congregations to function based on their core identity in the face of all eventualities. For example, rather than specifying that a "coffee hour" will take place each Sunday morning and setting forth all of the steps to make it happen, a congregation could covenant to be extravagantly welcoming toward members and visitors alike. That might result in continuing the coffee hour. But it might mean something else all together. And it might mean at times that the coffee hour doesn't happen if that's not where people's energy is and no one steps up to make it happen. Instead, something else might happen. Or it might not. Homemade pies might start mysteriously showing up early on Sundays, or fruit and vegetable platters, or something else surprising. And/or people might look beyond the Sunday morning block and organize dinners on Sunday afternoons or – dare we imagine? – on weeknights, in people's homes. The point is that when congregations are invested in a common purpose and freed from doing things the way they've always done them, new ideas can find their way into the life of the church, and they can bring new life by making things interesting rather than predictable.

When essential agreements are expressed in a form that people can even know by heart – in a simple rendering of what the congregation deems most important as it relates to the part of the overall ministry with which they are specifically involved – covenant guides can shift the responsibility for embodying the purpose of the church to the church's people seeking to faithfully live their church's ministry in every situation. Rather than creating a dynamic in which people feel burdened to "volunteer" for things they may or may not see as necessary or meaningful, providing more room for alternatives can create space for other possibilities that are not yet apparent but emerge organically from within and between the people who are your church at this time.

No doubt there is an underlying assumption at work here: that people are good and capable. In every congregation, important work is already being done by faithful people who are doing their best with what they've got. Stepping back from prescriptive bylaws and policy and procedure manuals begins with acknowledging the fundamental goodness of those around you. They are volunteering, after all. Indeed they have offered themselves to serve some greater connection. Something has moved them to risk becoming part of something larger than themselves. Step out of machine model thinking; people do not need to be pushed and prodded to do their work. They are not lifeless cogs in a machine but children of God looking to share their gifts and hoping to make a meaningful difference. Remember that people could be investing their energies and employing their talents somewhere other than church, which they have indeed chosen to serve. Notice what people are up to and work together to build processes that support and facilitate what is taking place. By all means, welcome the new ideas that are simply waiting for an opportunity to be made real.

Of course having people good-heartedly offer themselves for service does not mean that they will always agree on what to do or how to do it. Working through the challenge of doing complex things together can strengthen and reinforce bonds. Including different voices and opinions from the start of any endeavor can also enhance the work being done. Moving from many and varied starting places toward a shared common purpose can provide another opportunity to refine the congregation's understanding of itself in the world.

As you develop your congregation's Covenant Guide, think carefully about areas of ministry that are necessary to live the common purpose. With an eye toward simplicity, think about the general functions that might be needed to do the work you have set out to do. Do your best to set aside any notion you have of what you already do. Burn the pages on which what you have been doing is described, and remember that a little incense on the flame can add an air of holiness to the sacrificial offering. Instead, start again at the beginning, with a clean page, and imagine how you might organize now to do what you say you now do. Build in only what is needed to make your church strong, vital and stream-lined in the service of your shared commitment. As you move through the transformation, you might realize that you can beneficially re-align some existing groups and ministries to ensure their continued usefulness. But do that because it is necessary and not just for the sake of keeping them around.

Remember, too, that it really is OK to let things that seem to have lost their usefulness stop happening. Doing so can allow for a redistribution of resources toward functions that are more essential and pragmatically beneficial. And it can allow you to see if anything emerges to take the place of what is let go. Leave plenty of open space for people's passions to come to life, yielding new groups and programs that open still more possibilities. Former Coca Cola executive Donald R. Keough notes that, "Passion in one area sparks passion in other areas. It is contagious and leads to new ideas and new energy" (182). Before you know it, you might just find yourself waiting eagerly to see what happens next, who steps up to do what, and what gifts and passions they bring.

Covenant Guides invite and encourage congregations to consider the least restrictive, least prescriptive ways to live together toward the mission to which they are called. And they can move congregations toward organizational nimbleness.

On a practical level, Covenant Guides translate the common purpose into concise, two- to three-sentence summaries capable of providing general guidance to each identified ministry or group that is deemed necessary for the moment. Covenant Guides might then include some brief thoughts about what each ministry or group might address, but they stop far short of listing things to do or specific ways to do them. And they are best developed, of course, with as much involvement as possible by people who will actually be doing the work. In the end, each ministry or group has, at most, a one-page guideline, and all of the trust and support needed to make their work meaningful.

"Gatherings"

Is it fair to say that people generally do what they can to avoid meetings? The word itself can conjure up images of boredom, tedium, glazed over eyes, wasted time. I suspect that my daughters do as well as anyone at capturing the sheer despair even the mention of the word can arouse when they ask in utter exasperation if I have a meeting and desperately ask, "Do we have to go?" It's not that they don't like church or know that amazing things happen when committed people gather together. But they already know the monotony of meetings. And perceptions matter.

Reflecting on his time in leadership with the Coca-Cola Company, Keough notes that, "Meetings are the religious services of a great bureaucracy and the bureaucrats are fervently religious" (120).   It is hard, though perhaps not impossible, to find a person who would select being in a meeting as a favorite activity from among other reasonable options.

Let's step back for a moment... Why are there church meetings in the first place? Really. Why? Think about the last church meeting you attended. Was it necessary? Did it happen mostly because it was the second Wednesday of the month or the third Thursday or the fifth Friday? Did you do anything you could not have done more efficiently another way? Were there important things left undone because too much was brought up? It's not that meetings can't serve a very useful role in congregational life, but more that we need to think them through instead of taking them for granted as an inescapable burden of church leadership.

We've talked already about how systems need to connect with themselves in order to stay healthy and get healthier still. Getting together can indeed work toward very useful ends. But that isn't likely to happen like clockwork at a time designated by routine rather than need. Tim Brown notes that organizations need to be "always on... This capability is important because good ideas rarely come on schedule and may wither and die in the interlude between weekly meetings" (31). Imagine what might happen to them over the course of a month.

If meetings are thought of as points of contact that are essential for the system to thrive, it might just be that, at least for brief periods of time, they need to happen MORE often rather than less. But... But if they happen when they are needed they would presumably have a clearer focus than simply meeting because it's time. They might be more likely to yield results that create excitement and reinforce the usefulness of being together. Freed from routine, scheduled based on actual need, and focused on specific goals, they might even feel more purposeful and productive.

At the same time, people who lead meetings can exercise the option to not meet at a previously scheduled time if there is really nothing significant to be done.

In the context of churches as living systems, think of meetings as points of contact that are necessary for the system to thrive. Instead of "meeting," try "gathering," "connecting," "getting together." Or find another word that works better in your setting. This is more than a semantic change. Using different language can help change expectations and shape the process in constructive ways.

Think again about words like agendas and minutes. Those, too, conjure up a certain level of tedium and gear people to expect just that. Start with a "List of Things to Talk About" instead of an agenda. "Have conversations about things that matter" instead of "discussing items." Take "notes" rather than "minutes." Be creative and descriptive about what you are actually doing in ways that leave antiquated and stale language behind. And, in the process, change the culture in which your time together is immersed.

Make your time together useful by eliminating what does not serve a helpful purpose and building up those activities that work for a clear and greater good. Be stingy about topics and time; know that groups can be overwhelmed by too much information as well as by having too much to do. Allow time to go deeper into important topics. Eliminate "reports" that only rehearse what has already happened unless what happened was somehow especially remarkable. Be sure that what is shared is relevant for the context in which it is being shared. Ask whether your group needs to talk about something that another group, perhaps even one with considerably more first-hand knowledge and expertise, has already talked about and decided upon. Get past second-guessing that wastes time even as it dis-empowers those who are simply trying to do their work on behalf of all. Resist the impulse to micromanage; instead, trust the people on the ground in situations in which they are doing their best. And make sure that there is plenty of room in your gatherings to look ahead, and to imagine, and to dream together about the congregation you hope to become.

Look beneath what is customary to find opportunities to do something different. Change the meeting location. Just get together to talk. Or not; give silence its due. Wheatley calls silence "the pause that refreshes" (Finding 131). A few minutes here and there can allow time to collect thoughts and promote peace of mind. Make it a musical interlude, with recorded music or maybe the singing of a hymn. Light a candle and make time to watch the flame dance. Intentionally give God some floor time amidst the rush of whatever else feels pressing.

At its core, re-thinking meetings is again a process of examining what happens now, understanding why things happen like they do, and looking for alternatives that might even make it so that your time together is both useful and fun! Imagine the day that you are so excited about your next church board meeti…, er… gathering that you mark your calendar with a countdown that starts as far in advance as you know.

As Olsen points out, transforming meetings can capture that initial energy brought by incoming members and reinvigorate continuing members. More than that, it can reverse the trend that exists in some churches if not most where people serving the church in any capacity look forward to their terms being done, even as they think of reasons to "take a break" or never do it again.

It is often said that managers ask "Are we doing things right?" while leaders ask, "Are we doing the right things?" Leaders take a broader view which includes the possibility of doing different things. It is leadership that is the focus of this reflection. Leaders working within a living systems worldview have moved beyond command and control within hierarchical organizations to more collaborative leadership styles within emerging systems.

Leaders Not Bosses

"Leadership is dangerous" (Heifetz 235). One need look no further than the television show "Survivor" to know that one of the worst things that can happen to a person is being designated their tribe's leader. In the vernacular of the show, that designation more likely than not puts a "target" on leaders' backs and makes them more vulnerable to being voted off the island. Perhaps leadership in churches feels the same way sometimes.

Just as the world has changed, so have understandings of leadership and expectations of leaders. The world has, in many ways, turned up-side-down from the days when leaders authoritatively declared and people attentively listened, or when leaders charismatically cajoled and people faithfully followed. Remember that a key characteristic of living systems is that they are self-organizing with an emphasis on self. Wheatley notes that "Change doesn't happen from a leader announcing a plan. Change begins deep inside a system, when a few people notice something they will no longer tolerate, or respond to a dream of what's possible" (Turning 25). Emerging leaders harness that deep energy and commitment, then they help systems organize accordingly in a coherent way.

Hotchkiss reminds us that "In the most effective congregations, programs and ministries 'bubble up' continually from outside the formal leadership" (6). Grassroots movements make a difference. These days call for a new kind of leadership that both understands and values that.

Wheatley writes that leadership attends to "simple governing principles: guiding visions, sincere values, organizational beliefs – the few self-referential ideas individuals can use to shape their own behavior" (Leadership 130). Effective leaders work to keep people focused on the common purpose even as they continually work to bring that into clearer view. They help people say with clarity and resolve: "This is why we are here!" In the process, leaders ask questions that engage people in shaping their own behavior in the direction of that higher purpose. Rendle echoes Heifetz and many others in asserting that "leadership may be more about asking the right questions that can prompt new learning than about identifying and installing the next answer" (62).

As Kurtzman points out in the concluding statement of his book, in a section entitled "New Leaders, New Organization": "In the years ahead, leaders who can create common purpose will be in great demand. These leaders are likely to be kinder, more caring, and more empathic than leaders in the past. And by connecting with people on their teams at a human and purpose level, they are likely to create organizations superior to anything that has come before" (195).

Wheatley notes that, "In this chaotic world, we need leaders. But we don't need bosses. We need leaders to help us develop the clear identity that lights the dark moments of confusion. We need leaders to support us as we learn how to live by our own values. We need leaders to understand that we are best controlled by concepts that invite our participation, not policies and procedures that curtail our contributions" (Leadership 131). Leadership styles are changing at the same time as the world in which leadership is practiced changes. Can the church afford to miss a step?

Adaptive Versus Technical Work

In his book *Leadership Without Easy Answers*, Harvard professor and leadership guru Ronald Heifetz makes the distinction between technical and adaptive challenges. Essentially, technical work is required when a situation is well-understood and the solution is relatively straightforward. It involves drawing on and employing what is already known. Adaptive work, on the other hand, is required when either the problem or the solution or both are unknown and the situation calls for new ways of thinking.

Using physician-patient relationships as an example, Heifetz (76) describes three situational types to explain the difference between technical and adaptive work. Type I situations involve clear problem definitions and clear solution and implementation. Type I situations call for technical work in which the physician does a commonly recommended intervention that cures the patient. Type II situations involve clear problem definition but unclear solution and implementation. In that case, understanding the problem is straightforward while formulating the solution requires a new, adaptive way of thinking about the problem. Type III situations involve both problem definitions and solutions that require a new way of thinking.

In a church context, if the boiler breaks and the heating system shuts down, and if there is a known and achievable fix for the problem, the challenge is technical. If the boiler breaks and there is no way to fix it or pay for repair or replacement, the challenge becomes adaptive, requiring a new way to imagine and implement a novel solution.

Heifetz suggests a "key differentiating question" (87) to determine whether a problem requires technical or adaptive change: "Does making progress on this problem require changes in people's values, attitudes, or habits of behavior?" If it does, the called-for solution is adaptive.

One of the potential pitfalls of leadership is applying technical solutions to what are really adaptive problems. Increasing church attendance, for example, might appear to require a technical fix; a campaign can be mounted to get more people in church. But underlying the apparent technical problem can be issues that require an adaptive approach, issues like changes in the culture regarding church attendance, shifts in the congregational culture, or a host of other possibilities. Inappropriately applying the quick fix of a membership drive can fall short of expectations, prompt a wave of worry when such an intervention doesn't work, and end up frustrating those involved in trying to make it happen.

We are now in a time when churches and church leaders are facing adaptive challenges relative to all of the ways the world has changed and is changing. Consequently, nearly every significant decision churches have to make requires changes in values, attitudes, or habits of behavior. Adapting is the vital challenge.

C. Kirk Hadaway poignantly reminds us that "hard problems are not simple; they are hard. Making our problems appear to be simple and working on simple solutions keeps us from working on real solutions" (16). That is exactly what happens when we try to apply technical solutions to adaptive challenges. Senge and his team (in the Resource Reflection section) are helpful here in reminding us that we need to delve deeper together into understanding current realities and discovering new ways forward. Doing so requires making and taking the time to stop and think.

Heifetz writes that, "Because making progress on adaptive problems requires learning, the task of leadership consists of choreographing and directing learning processes in an organization or community. Progress often demands new ideas and innovation. As well, it often demands changes in people's attitudes and behaviors. Adaptive work consists of the process of discovering and making those changes" (187). At a most basic level, leaders need first to restrain themselves from attempting to rush in with "solutions" to problems. At the same time, there can be great benefit if they ask questions, re-frame problems, or otherwise engage all participants in understanding the nature of the situation they are encountering together.

Because organizational learning builds upon itself, facilitative leadership activities can work toward creating a learning environment that can benefit the immediate situation and be drawn upon to deal with future challenges.

Strategies can be utilized like "getting on the balcony" (Heifetz 252) which involves taking a step back to get an overview of what's going on, and, as mentioned earlier, attending to "creative deviants" (183) who are not yet co-opted into the system and who may yet have fresh insight to offer.

A Sampling of Leadership Ideas

Kurtzman writes that "It turns out that the people who are the most effective leaders are those who bring out the best in others "(171). That can happen in a number of ways, ranging from individual interactions with others in the organization to grand strategies that affect the whole organization at once.

Walt Disney is famous for appreciating good work done by his employees – and then telling them to "plus it" – to take it one more step to make it even better. That was part of his push to help people – and the company – be the best they could be. Where else but in churches should we be "plussing it," going that extra step, constantly striving for the next level? And "plussing it" is a way of validating people by acknowledging and possibly uncovering as yet unrealized potential.

Disney also saw himself as a "bee," whose role was to carry information between various components of the organization. Sawyer points out that, in the absence of centralized hierarchical authority that comprised earlier business models, it is useful for organizations to have a person who "is a catalyst and facilitator, acting as a connector between groups, a cross-pollinator and carrier of knowledge" (173). That function can be carried out by all people involved in congregational leadership.

Keough writes that, "As president of The Coca-Cola Company, I always described myself as a high-priced janitor.

My job was to keep the aisles clear so that our brightest associates could get their jobs done" (124). Doing so, of course, requires humility.

Benjamin Zander, in The *Art of Possibility*, takes a different approach. Troubled by the effect of what he calls "The World of Measurement" (17) on his students' performance, Zander developed the strategy of giving each of his students an "A" at the outset of each course. That way they were freed from the stress of evaluation and assessment which are so closely linked with the world of measurement and often precipitate fear which drives down performance and inhibits creativity. As a result of getting an "A," students were able to enter what he calls "A Universe of Possibility" (19). There, he notes, "unimpeded on a daily basis by the concern for survival, free from the generalized assumption of scarcity, a person stands in the great space of possibility in a posture of openness, with an unfettered imagination for what can be." What a grand and glorious place to be!

In giving an A to his students, Zander initiates a powerful shift in the dynamic between teacher and student, one that "allows the teacher to line up with her students in their efforts to produce the outcome, rather than lining up with the standards against these students" (33). In congregational systems, there is that same choice, whether to align with the people doing the work and ministry of the church or with the established structures and official policies and procedures. In terms of leadership for a new age, aligning with people is much to be preferred.

Perhaps most important of all, leaders live the common purpose and reflect it in what they themselves actually do. Decades ago, W. Timothy Galway wrote a series of books called "The Inner Game" of various sports. When he wrote about teaching people to do things like hit tennis balls or drive golf balls, he suggested that the best method was to invite students to simply observe someone doing it right. Words can only complicate things and telling people to "Do what I say and not what I do" leaves much to be desired on many levels, including educational. Effective leaders live the common purpose.

There are open questions, of course, about what the future will hold for churches as organizations. Who can know what will become of leadership, or how expectations of leaders will evolve? Congregations now, it seems, have mostly negotiated the transition away from the days of authoritative pastoral leadership, and pastors have mostly done the same. We have been in an era in which shared leadership was talked about, experimented with, and largely put in place. A living systems approach to church organization calls for yet another shift in church life and leadership, one that highlights emergent ideas and passions, recognizes the power of the people, and perhaps gives churches another chance to rediscover God in the mix.

Senge and his colleagues give us a glimpse into the future from where they now stand. "The leadership of the future will not be provided simply by individuals but by groups, institutions, communities, and networks... the future can emerge within the group itself, not embodied in a 'hero' or traditional 'leader.' I think that this is the key going forward – that we have to nurture a new form of leadership that doesn't depend on extraordinary individuals" (191). Instead we all have the potential, and the responsibility, to make meaningful contributions to the life we share.[5]

Wheatley lifts up the words of South American poet Machados: "The road is your footsteps, nothing else" (Finding

---

[5] Shared leadership has implications for pastoral evaluations, if such evaluations are done at all. Rather than designing and using tools focused solely on pastoral performance, evaluations can be developed and adapted to allow for a more systemic look at church functioning. Such systemic evaluations derive from the common purpose and include some assessment of pastor, congregation, and self on identified dimensions. They also include the names of respondents rather than allowing anonymous ratings and comments; in so doing they create a context for understanding and follow-up conversation.

43).[6] Rendle reminds us that "There are few straight steps in the wilderness, which is why it is called a wandering" (18). What a frightening prospect. Yet what an awesome invitation... Those words together reaffirm Heifetz' notion about leadership being dangerous. In turn, they compel us to summon our courage and take the next step lest we fall hopelessly out of pace with a world that keeps moving forward.

Pastoral and Prophetic Leadership

As we think about church leadership for a new age, we might finally consider the continuum on which church leadership uniquely exists. Pastoral leadership, on one end of the continuum, attends primarily to the needs of the congregation and its members while prophetic leadership on the other end reaches beyond the congregation into the wider world. While there is always a need to balance those two aspects of church leadership, we can be reminded that Jesus leaned toward justice in the wider world. Pastors and congregations do well to remember that tipping toward justice is part of the highest calling for churches and their leaders. Jesus was a prophet for all, not a chaplain for a few. Shall we follow his lead?

---

[6] The Grateful Dead, in "Ripple," also sing about leadership dynamics in a way that promotes conversation about leadership, followership, risk, impact. The song, with printed lyrics, can prompt meaningful conversation about leadership in your setting.

15) TINKERING TENACIOUSLY

Singer Harry Chapin wrote a song called "Flowers Are Red" that raises a poignant critique of the way education has sometimes played out. The song tells the story of a little boy who goes to the first day of school and paints flowers that are all different colors. The teacher says it's not time for art and, after a brief lecture on conformity, adds sternly that, "Flowers are red, young man, and green leaves are green. There's no need to see flowers any other way than the way they always have been seen." The little boy responds delightedly, "There are so many colors in the rainbow, so many colors in the morning sun, so many colors in a flower and I see every one." At first he pleads his case and stands firm, but eventually the little boy gives in. Then one day he moves to a new school where the smiling new teacher invites him to use all of the colors when he paints flowers. He replies using his former teacher's stern words and in a voice that is a mere echo of his former self, "Flowers are red, and green leaves are green. There's no need to see flowers any other way than the way they always have been seen." The story ends with a hope that all children will one day sing instead, "There are so many colors in a rainbow, so many colors in the morning sun, so many colors in a flower and I see every one."

I hope the little boy got his colors back... But the world can be pretty stifling sometimes. So can the church, at least by reputation. There are "right" ways and "wrong" ways to do things, "proper" ways to organize, "good" and "bad" results. And, with various degrees of emphasis depending upon one's theology, eternal damnation remains a constant threat for not getting it right. Growing up in that kind of world can be tough on a person and create so much pressure. Philip Yancey, in *What's So Amazing About Grace*, writes of a friend who, engaged in a street ministry, encountered a young woman who was in dire straits. He suggested that she try attending a church. She responded by asking, "Why would I ever go there? I was already feeling terrible about myself. They'd just make me feel worse" (11). Sadly, I fear that the woman is not alone in that perception.

Yet there is another side to human nature, a side that never forgot, a side that still cherishes the playfulness and sense of adventure that is part and parcel of being a child and maintaining child-like wonder. Wheatley ponders the difference between the ways children throw themselves off balance on purpose, by swinging and jumping and flying through the air, but adults, not so much. What happens to change (many of) us along the way? What do we miss out on as a result? Of course the answers have direct bearing on church organization.

Gary and Kim Schockley, in their book *Imagining Church: Seeing Hope in a World of Change*, remind us that "we must learn to paint outside the lines, take some risks, stop being afraid to mess up the picture, and begin to experience for ourselves a new opportunity to work with the Divine" (28). A former therapist once recommended that I learn how to manage my worries by going to a playground and watching children play. It was a remarkably healing thing to do. It reminded me of what it means to be care-free and spontaneous. You might try it.

Philosopher Martin Buber said this: "I cannot accept any absolute formulas for living. No preconceived code can see ahead to everything that can happen in a man's life. As we live, we grow and our beliefs change. They must change. So I think we should live with this constant discovery. We should be open to this adventure in heightened awareness of living. We should stake our whole existence on our willingness to explore and experience" (qtd. in Hodes 1972). Constant discovery... adventure... willingness to explore... Would you claim any of those as accurate descriptors of your congregation's organizational life? Do you think it would be good if you could?

A Culture of Experimentation

Rather than maintaining predictability and stability, Tim Brown claims that, "It is better to take an experimental approach: share processes, encourage the collective ownership of ideas, and enable teams to learn from one another" (17). It is easier, perhaps, to imagine taking such an approach in design studios than in congregations. But that doesn't mean that an experimental culture can't be appropriated meaningfully for church life.

To begin with, such a culture has as its base the recognition that it is better to ask forgiveness afterward (something familiar to churches, to be sure) than it is to ask permission before. (OK, go ahead and let out that audible gasp.) Brown notes that, "A culture that believes that it is better to ask forgiveness *afterward* rather than permission *before*, that rewards people for success but gives them permission to fail, has removed one of the obstacles to the formation of new ideas" (32). If people are afraid to do anything, nothing will happen. And I don't think God intends churches to be places for people to get together and do nothing.

Remember that there is a difference between thinking about things in theory and living them in reality. On a conceptual level, the thought of embracing experimentation as a part of congregational life might seem jarring in some ways. But think about the countless ways people already live that way in congregations, making choices that make sense in the moment, doing what it takes to get things done. Part of the challenge is simply acknowledging that we're at least part of the way to an experimental culture already. We can't help but be. The question is whether we can claim it openly and have it become part of how we think about ourselves.

Developing new ideas is risky business in the sense that not all new ideas work out as planned. Not all trials are successful. There are, of course, absolutely no guarantees that everything is going to work smoothly. But that is the nature of both the world in which we live, and the process of change. Here's how I see it: Congregations need new ways of organizing that account for the ways the world has changed and is changing. New ways of organizing require new ideas. New ideas will be accompanied by mistakes and failures. So if we're going to get to where we're going, we'd better be prepared for things to be messy.

If I were approaching this from a machine model perspective, I would surely wish there were a way to sugar coat that. If the world is on a track toward inevitable deterioration and death, as Newton would have us believe, and if Darwin is right that only the fittest survive, introducing mistakes and failures into a system that can still claim at least some semblance of equilibrium would justifiably be considered utterly foolish. However, if, based on billions of years of experience, life is all working toward more abundant life, and if that process sometimes requires even massive disruption on the way to better life, the risk – the choice, the possibility – of welcoming mistakes and failure as part of an ongoing learning process becomes a lot more compelling. One might even think of it as necessary, not just as a means of avoiding death, but as the only path to new life.

That said, you and your congregation surely have a choice. You can still choose to hunker down in fear of the disruption and chaos generated by mistakes and failures and the uncertainty brought on by change itself. Better the devil you know, right? Or you can trust that the disruption and chaos that come with change will help your church become the church you are waiting for – the church the world is waiting for.

What if you choose change? Brown writes that, "To be creative, a place does not have to be crazy, kooky, and located in northern California. What *is* a prerequisite is an environment – social but also spatial – in which people know they can experiment, take risks, and explore the full range of their faculties" (32). Cultures of experimentation encourage risk-taking. They risk both failure and success. They risk change. They welcome and even recruit people willing to see things differently, share novel ideas, test limits. They seize learning opportunities and silence critics waiting to assign blame when things don't work. Wheatley asserts that "It takes a lot of contributions from many people to create failure. We're wasting the opportunity to learn and grow if we try to pin the blame on just one person or one reason" (Perseverance 67). In organizations that create a culture of experimentation, everyone ought to feel equally entitled to claim credit for what happens, for better or worse.

Donald Keough, who was in senior management at the Coca Cola Company when the "New Coke" was introduced reflects on that and the Edsel and 45rpm records by noting that "these failures... are simply risks that just didn't work out" (23). Esslinger adds that "When you want to be the best, you can't be dogmatic... When something works well, you try to get better at it; when something goes wrong you learn from it, and move on" (40).

When I first arrived at my current church, I felt called to begin a yearly Easter Vigil service. I had always experienced the order for that service personally as an example of the grandest liturgical drama. The first year we did it, about forty people came – a nice crowd for a new and unfamiliar service. The next year, the number cut in half. In the third year, the number dropped to three people aside from the choir that had worked for weeks preparing the music for the service. Though the Easter Vigil remains a wonderful service in its own right, it was not attempted again in subsequent years. Though attendance was not a singularly defining factor, the number of attendees did not justify the extensive use of resources, especially in light of informal feedback that high liturgy did not appeal to many members or potential guests. It was initially worth trying even though it eventually became necessary to give it up.

It would seem that creating an experimental culture would also benefit from recalling Ogle's smart world that operates by making connections between disparate idea spaces; freeing our minds to explore new ideas, even if they initially seem bizarre, might lead us to breakthrough creativity.

Ogle even claims tinkering as a sort of default mechanism for bringing about break-through creativity when he notes that "If creating is often indistinguishable from finding, then navigation skills are the key... Linear thinking travels one link at a time. Accidents, analogy, and tinkering can all be exploited to break free from such bounds. They can directly link two widely separated areas of a web of ideas without any concern for the myriad low-level intervening links, thereby short-circuiting the connecting process and so saving creative energy" (159). In short, tinkerers sometimes get lucky and save themselves a lot of work in the process.

Rendle quotes a Native American saying: "Stumbling is moving ahead faster" (32).

Practicing Prototyping

I have previously written that prototyping is perhaps the most significant practical lesson churches can learn from design thinkers. It is a way of moving from ideas to models that in turn help us generate better models and new ideas. Tim Brown states that, "prototyping at work is giving form to an idea, allowing us to learn from it, evaluate it against others, and improve upon it" (94). Ideally, each "iteration" moves closer to the desired result. Churches can access the power of prototyping in the process of organizational redesign, as well as in other aspects of their daily life together.

Prototyping helps solve the problem illustrated by the comic strip that has people encountering a sign post with an arrow pointing one way to "Heaven" and another arrow pointing the other way to "A Discussion about Heaven." Of course the people are shown walking down the path toward the discussion. Church people have a knack for talking the life out of good ideas. Prototyping helps avoid that potential pitfall.

No doubt, talking is absolutely critical to church life. Conversation is vital and transformative and just plain helpful as we work to make sense of the life we share. But there does come a time when talking must give way to doing something. It is an art to know when that time has arrived, which is probably somewhere around the time the conversation turns to things that could as easily be tested as talked about. People stretching, yawning, snoring, all are also useful ways of knowing it's time for action or something different.

While design thinkers use such things as foam core and hot glue guns to prototype tangible products, experiences (e.g., developing a new meeting format, tracing the decision-making steps required for new ideas before they can be approved, etc.) can be prototyped by using such things as story boards where an ideal sequence is drawn out from start to finish, one step at a time. Ideas about interactional experiences can also be acted out by way of role-playing so that the process can be experienced, observed, and improved.

Organizational change is more challenging to prototype because there is really no way to fully remove it from the daily lives of real people (Brown 102). However, new ideas can be implemented as just that, new ideas. Having people involved in the experience can provide a wealth of information, especially if that information is deliberately sought and thoughtfully used. You might consider gathering in the church parking lot to capture the unique insights that environment seems to elicit, or planning a conference call so you can burn up the phone lines all together.

In the bylaws revision process described in a previous reflection, there came a time when the idea had to be enacted. The draft had to get "out of committee." The process leading up to the enactment was rich with opportunities for suggestions and modifications. The process following enactment carried on that spirit of constant modification. Putting the bylaws in effect was indeed a way of prototyping so that the document could continue to be adapted in meaningful ways – which it has and undoubtedly will be again.

In the end, Brown offers the reminder that "When it comes to organizations, constant change is inevitable and everything is a prototype" (105). In a fluid and ever-changing world, there is always something that comes next. In the same way that every program is a prototype, every pastor is an interim, and every congregation is well on its way to becoming something else.

Continuous Innovation

Brown's reminder is worth highlighting. There is never a time when innovation should stop in terms of organizational redesign. Design thinking is a continuous process; it is never once-and-for-all but ongoing. Roger Martin offers a conceptual framework called the "Knowledge Funnel" (6) that sheds light on how design thinking can foster perpetual innovation.

Essentially, new information enters the widest part of the funnel as mystery. It moves on to the next stage of the funnel as it is better understood. At that point it is labeled a "heuristic" (8) which simplifies the mystery and makes it more accessible and thereby more workable. If it can be even better understood it moves on to the third stage of the funnel where it is referred to as an "algorithm" (12) which provides an "explicit, step-by-step procedure for solving a problem." Martin sums up the process this way: "As understanding moves from mystery to heuristic to algorithm, extraneous information is pared away; the complexities of the world are mastered through simplification" (12). And, in the end, there is a simple formula or procedure to work with.

That is, however, the process for resolving only one mystery. Martin would suggest that organizations benefit from returning again and again to new mysteries that emerge, and that they keep striving to answer questions that linger or that were created by the last trip through the funnel. Instead of a one-trip journey, the knowledge funnel is intended for ongoing, repeated use. Brown points out that "innovation is not something that can be turned on and off like a faucet" (175). Instead, done well, it is a continuous flow.

Moving from mystery to algorithm once would be the equivalent, for example, of a congregation making a great big deal out of an effort at organizational redesign, calling in a big-time consultant, coming up with a product, and putting it in place for, say, the next ten or twenty or more years. Instead, as Esslinger puts it, "Without periodically tweaking its strategy, no business, no matter how successful it seems, is going to remain competitive in the long run. A truly excellent company is continually planting seeds for the future" (26). It would seem that the same can be said about excellent churches also.

It may be time for your congregation to tinker, or to tinker more. It might not. Psychiatrist M. Scott Peck once said this about change: "The truth is that our finest moments are most likely to occur when we are feeling deeply uncomfortable, unhappy, or unfulfilled. For it is only in such moments, propelled by our discomfort, that we are likely to step out of our ruts and start searching for different ways and truer answers." How are you feeling today?

SECTION FOUR: IMAGINING A WONDERFUL FUTURE

As this study draws to a close, the next two reflections help us to think through obstacles to creative innovation and establish means to sustain change through ongoing learning. One reading reminds us of the importance of hope and another summons us to reflect on why we do what we do. The closing chapter encourages celebration in the context of a joyful faith.

A church board, in order to accommodate rapid growth in their congregation and community, studied possible changes to their facility. After many months of conversation and consultation, the board recommended a renovation and construction plan that involved removing an historic altar that was highly valued by some but that hadn't been used during services for decades. While there was general support for the proposal, the board took a beating in multiple congregational meetings from some who were vehemently opposed. Long-time members threatened to leave the church. It was a very hard time for everyone involved. Even the pastor, who had been very careful to stay neutral through it all, had someone in a congregational meeting literally call for his head on a platter. Eventually, the project was overwhelmingly approved and the construction resulted in much-needed change that greatly enhanced the building functionally and aesthetically. But it was not easy to get there.

Such stories are dramatic and gripping. And there is a good chance that if you were to look back in your own congregation's history, you would find evidence of similarly intense battles about change. Maybe you don't need to look back very far at all.

In those situations, it's easy to frame the problem as resistance to change or resistance to authority, or resistance to something. But it may not always be that simple, if it ever really is.

Loss and Letting Go

Gil Rendle, in *Journey In the Wilderness*, is very helpful in drawing the connection between resistance and loss. He begins his chapter titled "The Jeremiah Moment: Moving Ahead Means Letting Go" with a story of a middle judicatory's organizational stream-lining that was met with fierce resistance because some people feared losing a seat at the table if there were fewer boards and committees (107).

Similar dramas are likely to play out in other denominational bodies as financial and other constraints affect the operations of central offices. Congregations coming to terms with fewer people and less money will also continue to face difficult choices about how to restructure their organizations to match available human and financial resources.

Heifetz and Linsky note that "People do not resist change, per se. People resist loss" (11). Loss can take many forms – loss of tradition, loss of familiarity, loss of power and esteem, etc. And because people tend to make uniquely personal commitments to churches, there can be an attendant sense of loss of self when congregations undergo change. Loss related to church life may go right to the heart of people's own sense of who they are.

People's responses to change can overwhelm and paralyze church systems. Rendle points out that, "At times the deep sense of loss and the reluctance to let go of what we know defeat the hope and possibility of change" (107). At the same time, Rendle notes, "Only when we are able to let go of what is lost can we claim and hold on to what is being offered" (108). That resonates with living systems understandings of giving up in order to grow, and it taps the theme of self-surrender that runs through Jesus' teachings and his life.

There are likely other common responses to situations in which people are understood as being resistant to change. The first is to pull back on proposed change in the interest of preserving a sense of congregational harmony in the spirit of being something like a happy family. Rendle is helpful here also in pointing out that "earlier assumptions of harmony now function effectively as norms to dampen needed new ideas and experimentation with new practices in the wilderness" (122). Yet all healthy organizations have differences and find ways to change and grow together without losing sight of the overall good.

A second way people and congregations might respond to resistance is by mounting a counter-resistance, meeting it head on with equal or greater political force. That is, obviously, likely to escalate tensions and decrease the likelihood of an affirmative resolution of the issues.

What might initially feel like a political battle turns out to be an opportunity for congregational self-care that might involve taking the time to talk about important things and work through the emotional aspects of loss and grief. Naming the loss and grief, taking the time to talk, and being sure to listen allows both speakers and hearers to be affected in ways that can be transformational. Taking the time to work through the process of change can also create opportunities to respectfully memorialize those things that are being lost.

Change is a totally natural part of life in living systems. But change requires that people engage in the work of adapting. That can be overwhelmingly challenging. If, for fifty years, I have been parking my car in the same spot on Sunday mornings and sitting in the same pew where my family sat since the church was built, I am going to have to make some serious adjustments, practically as well as emotionally, if the sanctuary is going to be redone and the construction is going to consume my parking spot. If, for decades, I have thought of my church as conservative, it makes some sense that I feel like "I'm always on the wrong side" of issues when the congregation takes a distinctly more liberal stance on important matters. That is also a time of loss and grief.

We have thought before about how machine-model systems respond to change with fear because change, viewed through that paradigm, can only move organizations closer to their demise. We have examined some of the ways change can threaten generational foundations and lead people to trepidation. Fear has been shown to actually limit people's ability to engage in imaginative thinking. Fear changes the way our brains work and brings mere survival to the fore. When Heifetz talks about creating holding environments (103) and regulating distress as a function of leadership (139), he is acknowledging the debilitating potential of stress within systems. Wheatley reminds us that "When we are overwhelmed or confused, our brains barely function. We reach for the old maps, the routine responses, what worked in the past. This is a predictable response, yet also suicidal" (Perseverance 39).

Even when you eventually need to forge ahead in accord with your congregation's common purpose, be sure to notice and create opportunities before, during, and after, to talk and to listen, to adapt what can be adapted, and to care for each other along the way. For example, a local congregation was considering whether to install video projection equipment in the beautiful, traditional-style Sanctuary. Multiple public gatherings on the subject allowed for the sharing of a variety of sometimes deeply-held and divergent opinions. The congregation eventually decided to approve the installation of the equipment. Those who disapproved asked for a second round of conversations about what the equipment would be used for. As a result of those gatherings, a mutually-agreed upon arrangement was made about the use of the system. In the end, all people were able to feel that they both had a say in the matter, and that they were heard – because they really were.

Challenging the Status Quo

Change situations arouse concerns about the system being knocked off balance, losing equilibrium. Yet Wheatley asserts that she has "observed the search for organizational equilibrium as a sure path to institutional death, a road to zero trafficked by fearful people" (Leadership 76). More than acknowledging the truth in that grim perspective, we do well to remember that challenging the status quo is built right into the foundation of Christian faith – though that is forgotten easily and often, as we thought about in the earlier reflection on church history. It is easy to get lulled into self-satisfied complacency.

Reading the gospels puts us in touch with the recorded stories about Jesus' encounters with Pharisees and Sadducees, those defenders of the established faith who pursued Jesus relentlessly, waving laws or bylaws or procedures manuals or whatever they could get their hands on. They gave him pop quizzes about matters of religion. They tried to catch him in inappropriate behavior and trick him into treason. They were forever criticizing his choice of dinner companions and friends. They seem to have deployed every technique they could think of to try to ensure that the way things were would be the way things stayed. Not only did they know the letter of the law, but they lived it, and advertised it, and made sure everyone around them knew that they knew. How much of their behavior do you think was motivated by fear of change? How much by an insistence on maintaining their positions of power within the system as it existed? How much by fear and sadness, or fear of sadness?

For his part, from the very beginning of his public ministry according to the recorded gospels, Jesus clearly came to challenge the established system. Of course that got him run out of town and eventually got him killed. Still, he turned the culture of his day upside-down by putting the last first and the first last, by redefining the status of poor and rich, women and men, children and adults. Jesus' mission was audacious. He paid attention to people and classes of people the rest of society had successfully managed to move to the margins. Remembering those stories reminds us that upsetting the status quo has been part of the Christian DNA for thousands of years now; it is our religious inheritance.

The Pharisees and Sadducees mounted a fierce, relentless, and overt attack. But then it doesn't take much to slow movement and even bring it to a halt; resistance sometimes shows up in more subtle and tentative forms that can also stop change in its tracks. On a trip back to Maryland from Pittsburgh, my girls and I got stuck in a traffic jam. It was not just a little delay but a massive stoppage of traffic. We sat for hours and I assumed that there must be construction or some major accident ahead. But in the hours that we waited, I took the opportunity to study the dynamics of traffic jams and discovered that something else was the culprit. In the occasional chances we had to actually pick up any speed before stopping again, I realized that brake lights really affect the flow of traffic, not only when people hit their brakes to stop, but when they flash their brake lights while they are moving at a good speed and the road in front of them is relatively clear. The effect of brake-tapping was that the next driver hit the brakes a little harder and the next a little harder than that, until we were eventually all stopped again. It's important to know what is causing slowdowns, and to proceed accordingly. Change depends on building momentum.

A Failure of Imagination

Even as he acknowledges imagination as "the mind's supreme faculty for dealing with the future" (113) and claims that it can be people's "most precious gift" (113), Ogle recognizes that, "Imagination has long had a bad rap" (68). That traces all the way back to Plato who prized reason over what might be viewed as mere flights of fancy (Egan 6). Nonetheless, imagination has, over time, found increased legitimacy. Kieran Egan, for example, notes that it "crucially involves our capacity to think of the possible rather than just the actual" (4). He writes that imagination occupies a powerful place "where perception, memory, idea generation, emotion, metaphor, and no doubt other labeled features of our lives, intersect and interact" (3). Paul Ricoeur goes even further in extolling the value of imagination when he claims that "imagination is par excellence, the instituting and constituting of what is humanly possible; in imagining possibilities, human beings act as prophets of their own existence" (qtd. in Harris 1)." Imagination isn't just kid's stuff any more.

Precisely because of that potential, imagination can be a powerful tool in the organizational life of churches. Yet it is often still relegated to secondary status or worse. In the midst of church board meetings in which we've engaged in imaginative exercises, I can imagine people thinking something like "OK, we played our little game. Now let's get down to the real work." I must confess to being guilty of such thoughts myself from time to time. But at what cost do we ignore the vast power of imagination? Reason is not the only way forward and numbers never tell the whole story.

In the widest scope, imagination is the foundation of faith. Unless you have had a face-to-face encounter with God, you, like the rest of us, are imagining God. Rather than worrying that such a claim diminishes faith, we might do well to embrace imagination as the profoundly spiritual act that it is.

William O. Avery and Beth Ann Gaede, in their book entitled *If This is the Way the World Works*, state that, "we cannot consider what we cannot imagine. Most pastors and parishioners cannot conceive of the congregation existing in any other form than the way we have known it. This viewpoint cripples their imagination, their ability to think of radically different models of the church in which diversity is a central tenet" (115). They offer this invitation: "We invite congregations to risk their own lives by considering different forms of the church that more easily incorporate diversity within them. And we urge congregations to remember that their lives do not depend ultimately on their competence, technical expertise, strategies, and long-term planning, but upon the power and faithfulness of God to raise the body of Christ from every death" (116). Imagine that.

17) LEARNING CONTINUOUSLY

Once I got used to it, I loved driving in Boston when I lived there. The experience inevitably turned out to be a way to both get where I was going and practice self-assertiveness at the same time. But even as I became more comfortable behind the wheel, rotaries continued to literally throw me for loops. There were three outcomes that weighed on my mind with every encounter with each new rotary. If all worked well, I thought, I would successfully negotiate the rotary and end up right where I meant to be. But the nightmare scenarios involved either being spun out at some random place and simply drifting off into the cosmic oort cloud, or being trapped in the inner lane of the rotary forever, never to be heard from again. Believe me when I say that I have vivid recollections of outright terror.

As was bound to happen, one day one of my nightmare scenarios played out. I thought I'd planned my entry well, positioning myself in what looked to be the correct lane. I grabbed the steering wheel with both hands and merged into traffic. If I could just move one lane to the left I would be on course for the exit I wanted. But, alas!, such a maneuver was not going to happen. Other drivers wouldn't let me in, even if they did know I was there, turn signal flashing, pleading for mercy as best I could at 30 miles per hour. I could do nothing but follow the lane I was in — which quickly diverted me to a place I'd never been before. A bit frazzled, I continued to look for a way back to the rotary where I could dare the fates again. But it turns out that the place I found to turn around was a beautiful park that I'd been hearing about but never visited because I didn't know where it was. And there it was, and there I was, where I wouldn't have been if I had managed to stay the course I had initially mapped out.

Given my discovery of a whole new part of the city, I was grateful that I was neither where I thought I'd be, nor stuck in perpetual circles in the inner lane of the loop. I reckoned that I was right where I was supposed to be, though not at all where I'd expected to be. So I took a relaxing walk around the park, and eventually continued on my journey, having learned something new along the way.

Learning involves new things. Otherwise, it's not learning. Newness defines learning. And learning never stops. We are forever being given opportunities to expand what we know.

One might be tempted to think of organizational redesign as an activity with well-defined starting and ending points, and a clock or calendar marking the time in between. It is as though locking in answers at a certain moment can finish the work until the next group takes up the task of reorganization when the congregation gets up the gumption to do it all again.

It is easy to assume that re-organizing involves a relatively isolated committee making a push for sweeping, across-the-board change all at once, followed by a much-ballyhooed "rollout," and a long period of living with what is developed and presented. But the world doesn't work that way. Why would we think church organization does?

As long as the world continues to change, church organization must be an open-ended activity. If we think of church reorganization as a matter of "getting there," we will discover that there is no "there" there. There is never a good stopping place because the finish line is always moving, constantly. Producing grand organizational redesigns is not a "Voila!" moment for any more than the precise moment a new plan or idea is introduced.

A new approach to church organization calls us to appreciate that organizational design is an ongoing learning process, not just decade-by-decade or even year-by-year, but moment-by-moment, not just traveling the roads and rotaries that we know, but venturing into new places – whether by choice or not.

Roger Swain, in *Saving Graces: Sojourns of a Backyard Biologist*, reports that he likes to walk the perimeter of his land at least once every year. Yet he confesses that, "The time, unfortunately, is hard to find. Like a woodchuck, I seldom venture far from one of the entrances of my residence. A hawk's-eye view of the farm would show the well-worn paths radiating from house and barn – paths to the vegetable garden, the compost heap, raspberry patch; paths to the woodpile, the orchard, vineyard, and sugarhouse. When our family decided to cultivate this bony land once more we little dreamed how it would shrink our horizons" (102). Learning calls us to step out of our ruts and routinely visit the boundaries of our land with fresh eyes.

No matter how prescient we are, we can only organize churches for right now. The further beyond right now that we attempt to organize, the more likely we are to have wasted time. It is entirely possible that any organizational design is obsolete the very moment it hits the paper it's printed on. Circumstances change. People change. The make-up of the congregation changes. The world changes. What else? Key members leave. Key members join. The roof caves in or the furnace breaks down. Mental telepathy replaces email as the newest way of communicating. Anything can happen to change what we think we know. Yet there is often pressure to design organizations to last forever. We can change that.

Peter Senge, founder of the Society for Organizational Learning offers this thought: In "learning organizations… people continually expand their capacity to create the results they truly desire, where new and expansive patterns of thinking are nurtured, where collective aspiration is set free, and where people are continually learning how to learn together" (Senge Fifth 3). Learning together takes commitment. And it takes time. But what is the alternative? And can you live with that?

QUESTION FOR REFLECTION: What might it mean to design a congregation that is for now and not forever?

Part and parcel of Zander's "world of measurement" are the myriad ways we measure and are measured by such things as "assessments, scales, standards, grades, and comparisons" (17). Zander notes that, "All the manifestations of the world of measurement... are based on a single assumption that is hidden from our awareness. The assumption is that life is about staying alive and making it through – surviving in a world of scarcity and peril" (18). That assumption is a lingering misperception from a world of machines that are thought to begin deteriorating from the very moment they begin to function.

Living systems thinkers see the world and life differently. Living systems exist in what Zander calls the "universe of possibility" (19) where actions are characterized as "generative, or giving, in all senses of the word – producing new life, creating new ideas, consciously endowing with meaning, contributing, yielding to the power of contexts" (20). Living systems understand life as working toward more abundant life by way of relationships that allow life to flow and change and grow. In short, "in the measurement world, you set a goal and strive for it. In the universe of possibility, you set the context and let life unfold" (21).

There was a tiny little church that trusted in new life. Once a thriving urban church, the architectural and cultural centerpiece of its neighborhood, the first church I served had become a mere shadow of its former self by the time I got there. But every Sunday morning, something like twenty hearty souls gathered for worship and fellowship, come rain or shine – but not necessarily snow. When the Sanctuary ceiling literally started falling in large plaster chunks around them, they simply put yellow "caution" tape on the pews in the particularly dangerous sections and worshiped where the plaster still seemed strong. Come winter, they were forced to move worship into the social hall, which was much smaller and cost a lot less to heat.

The people who brought that congregation to life were determined to maintain their connections with each other, with their neighborhood, and with the larger church. But their realities grew dimmer as the building continued to deteriorate and the remaining investments were barely enough to pay for even the basic winter utilities. It became increasingly clear that it was time for a radical decision. They could simply exhaust their resources and, when those were gone, they could walk away from their crumbling building. Or they could do a brand new thing. They opted for the latter – in a big way.

They dug down deep and discovered again their commitment to being a hospitable, progressive Christian presence in their neighborhood and for each other. They realized that their church was more than their building, and that the past was not a destination as much as a springboard to the future. They became the first officially Open and Affirming church in their half of the state and joined forces with a primarily gay and lesbian congregation with which they were familiar as a result of pioneering work done by a gifted former pastor.

And they did the unthinkable; they decided to sell their building that had become much more of a curse than a blessing. In coming to terms with that decision, people recounted many tales of past glory, and they remembered significant moments in the congregation's distinguished history. One eighty-nine year old woman made sure she took one last opportunity to stand in the very spot in the pastor's office where her mother had been baptized over a century before. There was much sadness in the letting go. And a fair amount of anxiety about how to move on. But faith won out, and new hope dawned.

The council president happened, through a chance encounter, to cross paths with a man looking to purchase and restore a building for use as his private art gallery and some possible development. He thought the massive church building would work perfectly. The deal worked out well for all, and it included a provision for church members to see the finished building when restoration was completed.

With a future now taking shape by the grace of God and the gutsiness of good and faithful people, they were also faced with a decision about where they would meet as a new congregation. While they were scouring the neighborhood for another location, and discovering that their neighborhood had become pricier than they had realized, they were offered use of the upper room of a funeral home – yes, a funeral home – that was still operated by a former church family whose main business had mostly moved to their suburban locations.

A mutually beneficial arrangement was worked out, and my last service as pastor of the little church seeking new life was to march them ceremoniously through the neighborhood, gold cross in hand, to the place from which their new life would emerge. Soon afterward, a "God is Still Speaking" banner appeared on the front of the building – right above the funeral home sign.

I'd like to report that new life came easily and that all things worked out as hoped. It did indeed, for a time. But eventually they were overwhelmed by the challenge of battling cultural shifts and sheer attrition. That said, I still look back with tremendous admiration for their willingness to reach toward new life by giving up most of what they thought they were for the sake of what they might become.

How many churches have or take the opportunity to wipe the slate clean and start all over again? There is something to be said for not really having much of a choice. But even then there is a choice. What would it be like if your church was able to start all over? Which aspects of the institution would be built back into the mix? What would be left behind? What serves life? What merely serves the institution for its own sake?

Sometimes, to be sure, moving toward more abundant life involves chaos and, paradoxically, even death. Leo Buscaglia, in his wonderful children's book *The Fall of Freddie the Leaf* reminds us that even death works toward life as autumn leaves fall to the ground to nourish the tree that will give birth to new leaves in a new spring. Moving toward more abundant life is an ongoing process of letting go of what has been, reaching out to what might be, and holding on just long enough to be able to start the whole process over again, and again, and again.

Living hopefully does not then mean looking at the world through rose-colored glasses, denying important realities, ignoring what is going on within us, between us, and around us. It means internalizing a basic sense of trust in the good for which all things work.

And living hopefully means acknowledging that expectations matter. If you expect a negative outcome, you will undoubtedly get an outcome that you can view as negative. If you expect that things are going to work out well, you will see instead the ways that things are working toward the end you hope for. The underlying dynamic is much like Gandhi's invitation to be the change you want to see in the world.

Believing in tomorrow makes it possible for churches to re-invent themselves today, whether driven by necessity, compelled by possibility, or both. A former United Church of Christ conference staff member is fond of pointing out that a number of churches in the area he served have been in existence since before 1776. He is intrigued by how many times those churches have had to re-invent themselves to still be around these centuries later.

Staying the same means falling behind in a world that's always changing. Moving ahead takes patience and great care, and faith that assures us that we need not be afraid. We live in a world of endless possibility and in the care of God who offers endless love and constant discovery.

A Practical Suggestion for Living Hopefully:
Stop counting everything! Churches can become obsessed with numbers (e.g., members, attendees, financial contributions, etc.). Numbers focus attention on whether there is "enough," most often leading to the conclusion that

there is not. Counting is blind to the workings of the Spirit, and it can generate needless anxiety that eventually makes "not enough" a self-fulfilling prophecy. Pay attention to quality not quantity.

EXERCISE:

Punctuate this phrase in a way that reflects your belief about your congregation's future:

Living Hopefully

(I will tell you that one clever person, when given the same exercise, thought out of the box and rendered this: Living Hope Fully. Is that an accurate descriptor of the way you live your life? Is it true of your congregation? How might it become more so?)

19) REFLECTING DEEPLY

Margaret Wheatley writes that, "In this historic moment, we live caught between a worldview that no longer works and a new one that seems too bizarre to contemplate" (169). We are between a machine model of organizational life that is well known but delivers at best only an illusion of control in an ever-changing world, and a living systems model that requires more trust and faith than we've had to muster but offers the promise of vitality beyond our wildest dreams. Negotiating this transition will require an honest examination of what we do, why we do it, and what is possible instead.

We have choices to make about how we will proceed, how we will organize our congregations for what we hope they'll be in the days and weeks and months and years and decades and centuries ahead. But it all starts right now. It is time to come to terms with the choices before us, and do what God is calling us to do in this moment.

Rubinstein and Firstenberg, relay a story from Ellen J. Langer about a family pot roast recipe. I offer it here as a reminder to guide your reflections. "The youngest woman [in a family] has always cut off a piece of pot roast before putting it in the pot. When asked by a friend why she does this, she realizes that she has no idea why it is necessary to cut off a slice, and calls her mother to inquire. Her mother is also puzzled by the question, and she tells her daughter that she cuts off a slice because that's the way her mother has always done it. They decide to question the grandmother on this ritual. The grandmother answers that the reason she slices the roast is, 'that's the only way it will fit into my pot.'" (12).

Why does your congregation do what it does? Have you thought it through lately? Have you explored options that might work better? This section is for you to sort some of that out on your own.

Take a look again at the table of contents as a list of topics we've reviewed together. Scan the section headings. And look at the practical suggestions included here. As you focus on each one, begin to develop a list of your take-away thoughts? I hope that you will think of this as a chance for a new beginning, full of opportunities and possibilities to be imagined and made real in the organizational life of your congregation.

MY TAKE-AWAY THOUGHTS:

_____

_____

_____

If you have been to Walt Disney World lately, you have undoubtedly been asked, "What are you celebrating today?" It is a poignant question that is part of a brilliant campaign to help make it so that the "Happiest Place on Earth" stays that way. The question appears as early in the vacation planning process as in the making of reservations: "Will you be celebrating anything while you're with us?" And there are big, bright, colorful buttons for seemingly every occasion — birthdays, anniversaries, first-time visits, etc. The celebrations set a tone that permeates the environment. (Think about the opposite, if, for example, all guests were asked "What are you worried about today?" I suspect that might have a different impact altogether.)

It's OK to feel good in church. Does your congregation have any claim to the title "Happiest Place on Earth?" Recognizing good things is not being prideful as much as it is the foundation for being grateful, and maybe even a little hopeful. J. Barrie Shepherd, in his wonderful book *Whatever Happened to Delight: Preaching the Gospel in Poetry and Parables*, describes life as a "treasure hunt" filled with delight (2). Believe it or not, delight even shows up in the organizational literature. Stephen Denning, for example, proposes a new model of "radical management" that is all about "pulling apart the black box of traditional management and putting the pieces together in a way that creates continuous innovation and client delight" (1). The approach maintains a focus on delight as its primary intention.

There is much to celebrate in every congregation. Celebrating your church's strengths may well be the next first step toward a new future built upon whatever it is your celebration lifts up. And celebration can take many forms, from large-scale festivals to simple words of appreciation for individual deeds. It can be ritualized, as in the formal celebration of a church anniversary, complete with a mass choir and representation from the wider church. Or it can be as free-form as the spontaneous gathering of a group at the local ice cream shop after finishing a meaningful project together.

As Paul Nixon reminds us, "The Bible is a joyful book. Christianity is an exuberant and happy faith" (Refuse 6). We have much to celebrate.

So what are you celebrating about your church today? How will you mark the occasion? And with whom?

_____

_____

_____

Summary

The way churches organize to do their work is as much a theological act as anything else they do, and it has impact on everything else they do. By setting aside outmoded, machine-based models of church organization and moving toward new models that are based on living systems, churches open themselves to new life. By discovering ways to organize nimbly, churches create opportunities to find God where God is and to seek God where God might otherwise be. Right now is the time for churches to make that choice. If staying the same means falling behind in a world that's always changing, the church must find a new way forward, now. That way forward summons the people who bring churches to life to engage with God in the act of co-creating a new church and a new world. God is waiting to amaze us. We will even surprise ourselves along the way. Are we ready to pay attention, and to join in the fun?

A Hopeful Affirmation

Years ago, my daughters had an old plastic wagon that we used to haul everything from baby dolls on their way to picnics on the beach to topsoil for filling holes in our yard. At the end of one summer I parked the wagon beside our house and tucked it neatly in what seemed a perfect winter storage place. But something strange happened the next Spring. It was a miracle of sorts.

Evidently, I had parked the wagon right over the spot where a plant intended to grow. Undaunted by its seemingly unfortunate location, the little plant sprouted up through a small hole in the bottom of the wagon. It grew where one might well have guessed it could not.

The sprouting of that little plant was not the plan of a master gardener. It was not the handiwork of a visionary horticulturist. Nor was it the product of careful attention that ensured that the shoots would find their way skyward or enough water would filter down to the roots. The sprouting of that plant was the creative work of God's world, achieving life against all odds by way of a force which draws life toward more abundant life.

Such miracles happen so often that we forget to remember that they are miracles nonetheless. Trees grow over rocks clinging precariously to hillsides. Rivers carve new pathways, forming magnificent canyons as they flow. Babies are born. Love is found. The sun rises and sets on each new day. And meaningful ministry emerges to inspire congregations and change the world.

In the beginning... God created. God is creating still, always and everywhere. And if we free ourselves from the woefully mistaken notion that we are the center of the universe and thus responsible for all that happens in it, if we, as the Psalmist says, still ourselves and let God be God, we just might, much to our amazement and marvel, be swept up in that process of creation that is going on all around us all the time.

PRESENCING

My high school history teacher had a poster on the corkboard above his desk. He pointed to it before every test. It said "Stop and Thnik." It was a simple reminder of what can go wrong when we don't.

But in the midst of busy lives, we neither stop nor think long enough to matter. This study is intended to provide an opportunity to stop and think about church organization, to see reality with clearer vision, and to move forward with clearer purpose.

Organizational consultant and educator Peter Senge was part of a marvelous collaboration with three others, C. Otto Scharmer, Joseph Jaworski, and Betty Sue Flowers. For more than a year, the four gathered occasionally to dialogue with each other, about their work, their personal experiences, the problems of the world, as well as some ways to make sense of what they were discovering and bring about transformation. Along the way they learned how to listen to each other, and to the present, and to the future. Their conversations and insights, recorded in their excellent book *Presence: Human Purpose and the Field of the Future*, help set the stage for what we are undertaking here.[7]

The team calls us first to stop, and to suspend our assumptions.

"In practice, suspension requires patience and a willingness not to impose pre-established frameworks or mental models on what we are seeing. If we can simply observe without forming conclusions as to what our observations mean and allow ourselves to sit with all the seemingly unrelated bits and pieces of information we see, fresh ways to understand a situation can eventually emerge"

---

[7] Scharmer presents a greatly expanded commentary on this work in his book *Theory U: Leading from the Future as it Emerges*.

(31). This study invites exploration of some of the bits and pieces of church organization and congregational life, and it urges suspension of assumed knowledge for the sake of potential learning.

The posture the team recommends conjures up images of Friedman's "non-anxious presence" which includes being "paradoxical, challenging (rather than saving), earthy, sometimes crazy, and even 'devilish'" (Friedman 209). Presencing calls us to playfulness rather than seriousness, to a spirit of discovery rather than a sense of premature certitude. The team's approach seems akin to a young child experiencing some aspect of the world for the very first time, free of preconceived notions and fully attentive to what emerges before her or his very eyes. Can you find your way back to that place?

Suspension is a necessary starting point for discovering who we are and who we are becoming. Suspending means clearing away our preconceptions and seeing the world for what it is. Suspending is the first step toward seeing the world again, not as an outsider, but from within, in a way that "dissolves the boundary between seer and seen" (43). On his *Bad Hair Day* album, Weird Al Yankovic wrote that, "Everything you know is wrong, black is white, up is down, short is long, and everything you thought was so important doesn't matter. Everything you know is wrong, just forget the words and sing along...." Suspending calls us to make room for the possibility that Weird Al was right.

Scharmer puts it another way. He claims that "it is only in our suspension of judgment that we can open ourselves up to wonder" (Scharmer 133). He adds that "Without the capacity for wonder, we will likely remain stuck in the prison of our mental constructs." Wonder liberates us and opens us to new, as-yet-unimagined possibilities. I hope you can bring a sense of wonder to this time and this process, not only wonder about how the world works, but about how models of congregational organization can usher in new realms of possibility.

But know this: Senge and the team caution that, "When we truly suspend taken-for-granted ways of seeing the world, what we start to see can be disorienting and disturbing, and strong emotions like fear and anger arise, which are hard to separate from what we see" (39). I once took a friend to get her first pair of eyeglasses for which she was long overdue. As we emerged from the optometrist's office, she looked up at the hillside across from the mall and said with amazement, "So that's what leaves on trees look like!" She was in awe of what she hadn't seen before. As we started driving home, however, her sense of awe gave way to a certain level of fear as objects she'd never seen in passing were passing by at a high rate of speed. Seeing the world more clearly, literally and metaphorically, has consequences that push us to the fluid boundary between excitement and terror. So get ready to be disoriented.

Senge and his team offer a process which they diagram as a "U" shape, with "sensing" being the primary task on the left side of the "U," "presencing" being the main work at the bottom of the "U," and "realizing" being the task of the right side of the "U."

Suspending creates the context for "sensing" which involves deploying the senses to "observe, observe, observe" (88). The risk in the sensing process is jumping too quickly to pre-established conclusions, while the goal is to go deeper, even becoming "one with the situation" (88). Sensing demands patience and a willingness to soak in all that the world offers the senses in a given moment.

Quoting economist Brian Arthur, the team points out that "presencing" requires getting to a place of "'inner knowing' where 'in a sense, there is no decision making. What to do just becomes obvious, and what is achieved 'depends on where you are coming from and who you are as a person'" (89). Being present in this usage means "becoming totally present – to the larger space or field around us, to an expanded sense of self, and, ultimately, to what is emerging through us" (91). It means being one with the world rather than separate from it, riding the wave instead of being overcome by it.

The right side of the "U" is committed to "realizing" which "involves bringing something new into reality" but "from a source that's deeper than the rational mind" (91). Just as entering the "U" through sensing required suspending what we thought we knew, so realizing requires restraining our will with regard to what to do next. Instead, what to do next becomes clear through the process, and realizing it is a deliberate act. It is not hampered by second-guessing or constrained by extensive planning, but acted on because it is obvious and authentic.

Moving from "presencing" to "realizing" is similar to when athletes enter what people sometimes talk about as being "in a zone." Their senses are heightened and their awareness is peaked such that baseball players, for example, talk about being able to see the individual threads on baseballs pitched at high speeds when they are batting. They become fully immersed in the context of the game and are thus capable of playing at their highest levels. Batters who are "in a zone" do not try to calculate the velocity or motion of pitches or think about the proper technique for swinging a bat. They simply let their bodies respond naturally, instinctively. They are not thinking about how to get into the game. They are playing the game from the inside. And in the process, they are freed to perform to their fullest potential.

In all things, the team reminds us that "there's an emerging future that depends upon us" (79), not separate from us but being "co-created" with us (92). When we are co-creating the future, the future is not happening to us but is instead emerging with and through us.

One of the team members, Otto Scharmer, in describing a process with which he had been involved, says, "There was a moment where 'the shared will and shared commitment of the group became clear to the group, when everyone knew why we were there and what they had to do. It was as if we saw deeply into the reality of our situation, from the inside of that reality. And in the seeing, we knew who we were and why we had come together'" (78). He adds that, "There was silence for a moment – not the absence of words but the presence of understanding." Perhaps the only way to know the potential this process bears is to work through it and get to that kind of understanding that is beyond words.

While the process as it's described lacks clear instructions – as it probably must, it offers the possibility of discerning shared understanding and common purpose. It seems worth engaging the process and trusting that that moment will come and that we will know it when we experience it.

Know too that this process is not once-and-for all but evolving like so much else we've studied here. The team calls for prototyping which is supported and shaped by continual and repeated immersion in the presencing process. They claim that, "the true nature of an emerging whole can't be accessed fully without engaging in concrete experiments, improvisation, and prototyping. What we begin to intuit starts to become clear and real for us in a totally new way once we consciously endeavor to make it manifest and stay open to the feedback that effort elicits" (150). Staying open to feedback from lived experience facilitates learning as an ongoing, never-ending process of experimentation and discovery.

CONVERSATION

Margaret Wheatley asserts that "we can change the world if we start listening to one another again. Simple, honest, human conversation. Not mediation, negotiation, problem-solving, debate, or public meetings. Simple, truthful conversation where we each have a chance to speak, we each feel heard, and we each listen well" (Turning 3). In important ways, conversation is an absolutely central element of the work that awaits congregations seeking new life. Conversation is worthy of being the last word in this study.

The way forward for congregations does not come about by way of trendy gimmicks or fancy tricks. It has nothing to do with flashy, high-priced consultants popping in with polished PowerPoint presentations of their latest greatest ideas about how things ought to be done. It involves much more than surface-level discussion used to decide on lists of things to do over the next year and five years and ten years. The way forward involves people really talking with one another about things that are important and coming to an awareness of what is possible as a result of the conversation.

Wheatley reminds us that, "if we can sit together and talk about what's important to us, we begin to come alive" (Turning 3). Others share similar sentiments. For example, Juanita Brown, one of the co-founders of World Café Conversations, states that, "It is still my deepest belief that it is through conversations around questions that matter that powerful capacities for evolving caring, collaborative learning, and committed action are engaged – at work, in communities, and at home" (2). Jamie and Maren Showkeir claim that "Establishing *new* conversations is the most effective way – and the most underutilized – to create ongoing, long-lasting change in our lives, our organizations, and society" (5). Meaningful conversation bears the promise of transforming people, and organizations, and the world.

Sadly, it has become somewhat of a lost art. Lives are busy and can easily become cluttered with distractions. Sometimes it is simply the pace of life that short-circuits opportunities to really talk with one another. While in some ways we are more "networked" than ever as a society, many of us feel more isolated and alone. Too often, it seems, differences divide us and can leave us feeling even more detached and less hopeful of connecting in meaningful ways.

Peter Block, in *Community: The Structure of Belonging*, notes that, "Ironically, we talk today of how small the world has become, with the shrinking effect of globalization, instant sharing of information, quick technology, workplaces that operate around the globe. Yet these do not necessarily create a sense of belonging" (1). Archbishop Desmund Tutu describes the current state of fragmentation in the world as "a radical brokenness in all existence" (qtd. in Wheatley Turning 4). But it has not always been this way.

Wheatley claims that, "for as long as we've been around as humans, as wandering bands of nomads or cave dwellers, we have sat together and shared experiences. We've painted on rock walls, recounted dreams and visions, told stories of the day, and generally felt comforted to be in the world together. When the world became fearsome, we came together. When the world called us to explore its edges, we journeyed together. Whatever we did, we did it together" (Turning 4). Somehow we have lost that sense of togetherness and belonging.

Conversation can help us find our way back together again. But it requires commitment and patience. It requires practice and a willingness to learn together. It requires being together and turning toward one another. Indeed Christina Baldwin and Ann Linnea, creators of PeerSpirit Circle Process, remind us of ancient gatherings in circles around fire pits where spoken language itself came into existence.

Conversation supports dialogue, "thinking together." It creates options for varying opinions to be conveyed in a way that makes shared understanding possible. And it can lift us out of loneliness into community. More than that, conversation bears the potential to bridge between even radically different perspectives in a world that has become more polarized, and it can work toward larger, over-arching truths.

Perhaps you remember the Gestalt drawing that could be perceived as either a chalice or two faces looking at each other. Some see it one way. Others see it the other way. The truth is that it is and always will be BOTH a chalice and faces. It might even be something else all together. Conversation makes it possible to develop a collective notion of what the drawing is.

There is a story, modified from its origins in the Jain tradition, about people who are asked to reach into various flaps in a tent and then to describe what they feel inside. One person reaches into the flap in front of him and assumes that he is touching a tree trunk, another a fly swatter, another a sharp spear, etc. It is only when they talk together and merge their perceptions that they realize that what is inside the tent is an elephant.

Craig Dykstra and Dorothy C. Bass describe a view of current reality that both invites attention to Christian practices, which is their focus, and at the same time seems to urge shared conversation as well: "Dislocated and disconnected, we suppose that *self*-help offers our best hope... The fact is that inward journeys are not enough to meet our need. Our lives are tangled up with everyone else's in ways beyond our knowing, 'caught,' as Martin Luther King, Jr. put it, 'in an inescapable network of mutuality, tied to a single garment of destiny'" (4). Might conversation be the most meaningful of Christian practices? It bears the potential of creating truly sacred space between people, bridging distances, building unity.

It matters that we are heard. It matters also that we listen. Wheatley states that "the act of listening brings us closer" (Finding 82). Yet it offers more than that. Simply being heard can provide powerful validation for each of our very existence. Dave Isay, founder of StoryCorps, has recorded thousands of interviews with people, and his book title defines listening as an act of love. He tells of one man who saw his interview written up and exclaimed "I exist! I exist!" (254). The possibility of that kind of affirmation makes conversation an even more powerful tool in reshaping church organization and working toward a better world.

Fred Rogers, in *The World According to Mr. Rogers: Important Things to Remember* says this: "Listening is where love begins: listening to ourselves and then to our neighbors" (93). This is based on his belief that "Listening is a very active awareness of the coming together of at least two lives. Listening, as far as I'm concerned, is certainly a prerequisite of love. One of the most essential ways of saying 'I love you' is being a receptive listener" (92). May we bring that spirit of love and that hope for connection to the conversations we will have both within and outside of our churches. And may God bless us in the talking and the hearing.

Some Ways to Talk Together

Life Story Collection

Life Story collection lets you start talking now instead of waiting until a crisis arises or there is an "issue" to address. To share life stories, create random pairings of people who are able and willing to talk one-on-one with another person. Ask each pair to find two hours to be together in a setting in which the distractions are minimized. For the first hour, have one person ask the other person simply, "How did you get to where you are?" and have the "interviewer" listen attentively to the unfolding story. For the second hour, reverse the roles. Listeners, most importantly, are to pay attention to what the other is saying. They might give affirming responses (e.g., nodding, saying "I see," etc.) or offer subtle prompts (e.g., "Can you tell me more about that?") but all in the service of helping the speaker tell the story of her or his own life. Interviewers will be most effective when they sit with silences and avoid rushing in to end them, but instead let speakers move on when they are ready and in whatever narrative direction they choose. In the end, have all of the participants talk together about the experience of listening and being heard. Remind people that they are not to report on what others said, but on their own response to being part of the sharing in both roles. Note how people and relationships are transformed by the process.

World Café Conversations

If you are seeking to create a dynamic context to generate ideas and capture thoughts in a group at a given moment, consider engaging in a World Café Conversation. This format allows you to address two or three major questions by intentionally inviting people to talk with each other. The process makes it so that people interact with each other as they continue conversations while rotating to different small groups. At the end of the final round of small group conversations, information is "harvested" and recorded in a large group format. An example of a particularly successful World Café process with which I have been involved was held at an annual association gathering, involving approximately forty-five people representing about thirty churches. Using the questions identified in an earlier reflection ("What do we know about ourselves right now?" and "What can we do now that we're together?"), the conversation helped us arrive at the basis for a statement of common purpose which was soon thereafter adopted. The definitive source for this model is *The World Café: Shaping Our Futures Through Conversations That Matter*, written by Juanita Brown and David Isaacs and published by Berrett-Kohler in 2005. Excellent resources are also available online at www.theworldcafe.com, including step-by-step instructions under the "Useful Information" tab.

PeerSpirit Circle Conversations

To create an environment for in-depth sharing, hold a PeerSpirit Circle Conversation. Beginning with the assumption that there is a leader in every chair, the authors outline a process that includes three specific kinds of conversations – talking stick council, conversation council, and silence council. In each type of council, time is deliberately taken to promote involvement by all participants who are willing to share. The intentionality of the councils is remarkably conducive to listening deeply to others, and it works in the service of people collecting their thoughts as they come together around important matters. Devote time and thought to the physical setting of your council; more information about this is shared in the book referenced below. As a review of a week-long course taught on this material, the group and I engaged in a talking stick council to name take-away lessons from the course. Every person had time to speak of their experiences. It was useful to also have the pauses built in by passing the talking stick around the group as people raised their hands to speak. In another example, a local congregation seeking to hear from members of the congregation organized an entire worship service in a circle and facilitated sharing by those who were willing. The central question was, "What do you celebrate about our congregation?" The service was so meaningful and moving that the church board decided to incorporate a circle time with various focus questions at the end of each of their gatherings. The PeerSpirit model was developed by Christina Baldwin and Anne Linnea, and is described more fully in their book, *The Circle Way: A Leader in Every Chair*, published by Berrett-Kohler in 2010. The authors also provide a wonderful array of resources online at www.peerspirit.com. Guidelines are provided under the tab "Circle Training" then "Circle Guidelines."

Six-Word Stories

If you would like to provide a way for people to boil down their experiences of a shared experience of everything from a discrete event to involvement with an ongoing organization, you might consider asking them to write six-word stories. The classic six-word story, which is perhaps erroneously attributed to Ernest Hemingway is, "Baby shoes: For sale. Never Worn." That example conveys some of the potential power in distilling stories to this format. There can be a great richness in the sharing of the stories. One congregation used this method to review three weeks during which they housed homeless people in their social hall. Each of the volunteers for the program presented a six-word story and key words were extracted to make a beautiful collage that now hangs in the hall. The process is fairly straightforward and ideas to support your work can be found online at such sites as www.sixwordstories.net.

"Yes, and..." Conversations

There is great power in the stories we tell together. "Yes, and..." conversations engage people in collective story telling in which each person's contribution is affirmed and then added to. Gather people in a circle and begin the story-telling with a short phrase that relates to your identified area of interest. For example, the first person might say, "The church of tomorrow will..." The second person, working around the circle, might then say, "Yes, and the church of tomorrow will welcome all people." The third person then might add, "Yes, and the church of tomorrow will welcome all people and care for the poor like Jesus did." The story then works its way around the circle with each person repeating what was said by the person before them and then adding something new. Some groups might be able to have participants repeat all of the responses before making their own contribution. If you are inclined to push past easy answers, go around the circle a second time; doing so requires people to dig deeper, and to perhaps be more creative in the process. The idea is to have all voices represented in the final story told by the group. That story can be written down or recorded and looked at to ascertain what things are important to the group.

Works Cited

Armstrong, Karen. *The Case for God*. New York: Knopf, 2009.

Avery, William O., and Beth Ann Gaede. *If This Is the Way the World Works: Science, Congregations, and Leadership*. Herndon, Virginia: Alban, 2007.

Bach, Richard. *Illusions: Adventures of a Reluctant Messiah*. New York: Dell, 1977.

Baldwin, Christina, and Ann Linnea. *The Circle Way: A Leader in Every Chair*. San Francisco: Berrett-Koehler, 2010.

Bass, Diana Butler. *Christianity for the Rest of Us: How the Neighborhood Church is Transforming Our Faith*. HarperSanFrancisco, 2006.
--- *The Practicing Congregation: Imagining a New Old Church*. Herndon,
　　　　Virginia: Alban, 2004.

Block, Peter. *Community: The Structure of Belonging*. San Francisco: Berrett-Koehler, 2008.

Brown, Juanita, and David Isaacs. *The World Café: Shaping Our Futures Through Conversations That Matter*. San Francisco: Berrett-Koehler, 2005.

Brown, Tim. *Change By Design: How Design Thinking Transforms Organizations and Inspires Innovation*. HarperCollins, 2009.

Buscaglia, Leo. *The Fall of Freddie the Leaf*. New Jersey: SLACK, Inc., 1982

Callahan, Kennon L. *Twelve Keys to an Effective Church*. San Francisco: Jossey-Bass, 1983.

Daft, R.L. *Organization Theory and Design* (10th ed.). Mason, Ohio: South-Western, 2010.

Denning, Stephen. *The Leader's Guide to Radical Management: Reinventing the Workplace for the 21st Century.* San Francisco: Jossey-Bass, 2010.

Dick, Dan R. *Bursting the Bubble: Rethinking Conventional Wisdom About Church Leadership.* Nashville: Abingdon, 2008.

Dykstra, Craig, and Dorothy C. Bass. "Times of Yearning, Practices of Faith." *Practicing Our Faith.* Ed. Dorothy C. Bass. San Francisco: Jossey-Bass, 1997.

Dykstra, Craig, and James Hudnut-Buemler. "The National Organizational Structures of Protestant Denominations: An Invitation to Conversation." *The Organizational Revolution: Presbyterians and American Denominationalism.* Ed. Milton Coulter, John Mulder, Louis Weeks. Louisville: John Knox, 1992.

Egan, Kieran. *Imagination in Teaching and Learning: The Middle School Years.* Chicago: University of Chicago, 1992.

Esslinger, Hartmut. *A Fine Line: How Design Strategies Are Shaping the Future of Business.* San Francisco: Jossey-Bass, 2009.

Friedman, Edwin H. *Generation to Generation: Family Process in Church and Synagogue.* New York: Guilford, 1985.

Galindo, Israel. *The Hidden Lives of Congregations: Discerning Church Dynamics.* Herndon, Virginia: Alban, 2004.

Goldstein, Jeffrey. *The Unshackled Organization: Facing the Challenge of Unpredictability Through Spontaneous Reorganization.* Portland, Oregon: Productivity Press, 1994.

Hadaway, C. Kirk. *Behold I Do a New Thing: Transforming Communities of Faith*. Cleveland: Pilgrim Press, 2001.

Harris, Maria. *Teaching and Religious Imagination: An Essay in the Theology of Teaching*. HarperSanFrancisco, 1987.
Heifetz, Ronald. *Leadership Without Easy Answers*. Cambridge, Massachusetts: Harvard University Press, 1994.

Heifetz, Ronald A., and Marty Linsky. *Leadership on the Line: Staying Alive Through the Dangers of Leading*. Boston: Harvard Business Review Press, 2002.

Hench, John. *Designing Disney: Imagineering and the Art of the Show*. New York: Disney Editions, 2003.

Hinson, E. Glenn. *The Church: Design for Survival*. Nashville: Broadman Press, 1967.

Hodes, A. *Encounter With Martin Buber*. London: Allen Lane, 1972

Holyoak, Keith J, and Paul Thagard. *Mental Leaps: Analogy in Creative Thought*. Cambridge, Massachusetts: MIT Press, 1995.

Hotchkiss, Dan. *Governance and Ministry: Re-thinking Board Leadership*. Herndon, Virginia: Alban, 2009.

Isay, Dave. *Listening as An Act of Love: A Celebration of American Life from the StoryCorps Project*. New York: Penguin, 2007.

Keough, Donald R. *The Ten Commandments for Business Failure*. New York: Penguin, 2008.

Kelley,Tom. *The Art of Innovation: Lessons in Creativity from IDEO, America's Leading Design Firm*. New York: Doubleday, 2001.

Kitchens, Jim. *The Postmodern Parish: New Ministry for a New Era*. Herndon, Virginia: Alban, 2003.

Kuhn, Thomas. *The Structure of Scientific Revolutions*. Chicago: University of Chicago Press, 1970.

Kurtzman, Joel. *Common Purpose: How Great Leaders Get Organizations to Achieve the Extraordinary*. San Francisco: Jossey-Bass, 2010.

Martin, Roger. *The Design of Business: Why Design Thinking is the Next*
        Competitive Advantage. Boston: Harvard Business Press, 2009.

McClintock Fulkerson, Mary. *Places of Redemption: Theology for a Worldly Church*. Oxford University Press, 2007.

McIntosh, Gary L. *One Church, Four Generations: Understanding and Reaching All Ages in Your Church*. Grand Rapids, Michigan: Baker Books, 2002.

National Council of Churches. *National Council of Churches Yearbook, 2009*. New York: National Council of Churches, 2009

Nixon, Paul. *I Refuse to Lead a Dying Church*. Cleveland: Pilgrim Press, 2007.

Ogle, Richard. *Smart World: Breakthrough Creativity and the New Science of Ideas*. Boston: Harvard Business School Press, 2007.

Olsen, Charles M. *Transforming Church Boards into Communities of Spiritual Leaders.* Herndon, Virginia: Alban, 1995.

Patton, Jeff. *If It Could Happen Here…: Turning the Small-Membership Church Around.* Nashville: Abingdon Press, 2002.

Pausch, Randy. *The Last Lecture.* New York: Hyperion, 2008.

Pew Forum on Religion and Public Life. "Religion Among the Millennials." 17 February 2010. Pew Research Center Publications. 16 Feb. 2011.

Powers, Bruce P. Ed. *Church Administration Handbook.* Nashville: Broadman and Holman, 1997.

Rasmus, Daniel W. *Management By Design: Applying Design Principles to the Work Experience.* New Jersey: Wiley and Sons, 2011.

Rendle, Gil. Journey *in the Wilderness: New Life for Mainline Churches.*
Nashville: Abingdon, 2010.

Robinson, Anthony. Transforming *Congregational Culture.*
Grand Rapids,
Michigan: Eerdmans, 2003.

Rogers, Fred. *The World According to Mr. Rogers: Important Things to*
Remember. New York: Hyperion, 2003.

Roof, Wade Clark. *Spiritual Marketplace: Baby Boomers and the Remaking of American Religion.* New Jersey: Princeton University Press, 1999.

Rubinstein, Moshe F., and Iris R, Firstenberg. *The Minding Organization: Bring the Future to the Present and Turn Creative Ideas into Business Solutions.* New York: Wiley and Sons, 1999.

Sanguin, Bruce. *The Emerging Church: A Model for Change and a Map for Renewal.* CopperHouse, 2008.

Sawyer, Keith. *Group Genius: The Creative Power of Collaboration.* New York: Basic Books, 2007.

Scharmer, C. Otto. *Theory U: Leading for the Future as it Emerges.* San Francisco: Berrett-Koehler, 2009.

Schieler, Robert D. *Revive Your Mainline Congregation: Prescriptions for Vital Church Life.* Cleveland: Pilgrim Press, 2003.

Schockley, Gary and Kim. *Imagining Church: Seeing Hope in a World of Change.* Herndon, Virginia: Alban, 2009.

Senge, Peter. *The Fifth Discipline: The Art and Practice of the Learning Organization.* New York: Doubleday, 2006.

Senge, Peter, and C. Otto Scharmer, Joseph Jaworski, Betty Sue Flowers. *Presence: Human Purpose and the Field of the Future.* Cambridge, Massachusetts: Society for Organizational Learning, 2004.

Shepherd, J. Barrie. *Whatever Happened to Delight?: Preaching the Gospel in Poetry and Parables.* Louisville: Westminster John Knox, 2006.

Showkier, Jamie and Maren. *Authentic Conversations: Moving From Manipulating to Truth and Commitment.* San Francisco: Berrett-Koehler, 2008.

Swain, Roger. *Saving Graces: Sojourns of a Backyard Biologist.* Boston: Little, Brown, 1991.

Truss, Lynne. *Eats, Shoots, and Leaves: The Zero Tolerance Approach to Punctuation.* New York: Gotham Books, 2003.

Verganti, Roberto. *Design-Driven Innovation: Changing the Rules of Competition By Radically Innovating What Things Mean.* Boston: Harvard Business School, 2009.

Wheatley, Margaret J. *Finding Our Way: Leadership For an Uncertain Future.* San Francisco: Berrett-Koehler, 2007.
--- *Leadership and the New Science: Discovering Order in a Chaotic World.* San Francisco: Berrett-Koehler, 2006.
--- *Perseverance.* Provo, Utah: Berkana, 2010
--- *Turning To One Another: Simple Conversations to Restore Hope to the Future.* San Francisco: Berrett-Koehler, 2002.

Wink, Walter. *Engaging the Powers: Discernment and Resistance in a World of Domination.* Minneapolis: Fortress Press, 1992.

Yancey,Philip. *What's So Amazing About Grace?* Michigan: Zondervan, 1998.

Zander, Rosamund Stone, and Benjamin. *The Art of Possibility: Transforming Professional and Personal Life.* New York: Penguin, 2000.

About the Author

Rev. Dr. Marty Kuchma is Senior Pastor of St. Paul's United Church of Christ, Westminster, Maryland. He is also Adjunct Faculty at Lancaster Seminary where he leads the first-year Doctor of Ministry Seminar and teaches occasional courses on church leadership, organizational dynamics, and revitalization and renewal. He has received a Bachelor of Arts from St. Vincent College in Latrobe, Pennsylvania, a Master of Social Work from the University of Pittsburgh, a Master of Divinity from Andover Newton Theological School in Newton Centre, Massachusetts, and a Doctor of Ministry from Lancaster Theological Seminary in Pennsylvania.

He is reachable by email at churchbenimble@gmail.com and is available for presentations, workshops, and consultations depending on timing and travel requirements.

More information is available at www.churchbenimble.com.